**W9-APR-605**

THE GREAT HISPANIC HERITAGE

Roberto Clemente

THE GREAT HISPANIC HERITAGE

THE GREAT
HISPANIC HERITAGE

Roberto Clemente

Susan Muaddi Darraj and Rob Maaddi

CHELSEA HOUSE
PUBLISHERS
An imprint of Infobase Publishing

Roberto Clemente

Copyright © 2008 by Infobase Publishing

Chelsea House
An imprint of Infobase Publishing
132 West 31st Street
New York NY 10001

Library of Congress Cataloging-in-Publication Data

Maaddi, Rob.
  Roberto Clemente / Rob Maaddi and Susan Muaddi Darraj.
    p. cm. — (The great Hispanic heritage)
  Includes bibliographical references and index.
  ISBN 978-0-7910-9691-8 (hardcover)
  1. Clemente, Roberto, 1934-1972. 2. Baseball players—Puerto Rico—Biography.
I. Darraj, Susan Muaddi. II. Title. III. Series.
  GV865.C45M323 2008
  796.357092—dc22
  [B]   2007032077

Contents

Turning Pro

Each day Roberto Clemente came to the ballpark during his first year in professional baseball, he would have to check the lineup card to see if he was playing. No matter how well or how poorly he performed the previous game, Clemente was not guaranteed a spot in the starting lineup with the Montreal Royals. The reasoning was more complex than simply a matter of skills.

Playing for Santurce in the Puerto Rican Winter League in 1952–1953, 18-year-old Clemente had an outstanding season. He batted .356 and was so impressive at an earlier tryout clinic that scout Al Campanis offered the strong-armed outfielder a $10,000 bonus to sign with the Brooklyn Dodgers in the major leagues.

Clemente had to finish high school before he could sign with a major league team, but he verbally accepted Campanis's offer. Before he graduated, other teams offered

Clemente more money to sign with them. It was reported that the Milwaukee Braves were willing to triple Brooklyn's signing bonus and offer close to $30,000. Clemente was a man of his word, however, and he signed with the Dodgers. "He was the best free-agent athlete I have ever seen," Campanis once said.

The Dodgers had a star-studded outfield featuring three players who were on the National League's All-Star team in 1953: Carl Furillo, Duke Snider, and Jackie Robinson. They also had a promising player in the minor leagues, Sandy Amoros, who led the International League in hitting with a .353 average.

With all this outfield talent available to them, why were the Dodgers so eager to sign Clemente? Many baseball insiders speculated that the Dodgers wanted to prevent their crosstown rival, the New York Giants, from getting Clemente. Whatever the reason, Brooklyn management knew it would be tough for Clemente to break into the majors as a teenager. They assigned Clemente to the Dodgers' Triple-A minor league team, the Montreal Royals.

It was a huge risk for the Dodgers because major league rules stated that a player who received a bonus, including salary, of more than $4,000 must be kept on the major league roster for two years or be eligible for a postseason draft. Campanis warned Dodgers vice president Buzzie Bavasi about gambling on Clemente, but there simply was no room for him with the talent-packed Dodgers team.

Many biographers maintain that the Dodgers tried to hide Clemente from the watchful eyes of other teams by assigning him to Montreal and giving him limited playing time. Though some claims have been disputed, such as one that said Clemente was benched a day after hitting three triples in one game, he did not play regularly that season with Montreal. Another reason for his lack of playing time could have been that the Royals already had a crowded outfield that included Dick Whitman, Gino Cimoli, and Jack Cassini. Clemente was

Roberto Clemente played his entire 18-year Major League Baseball career for the Pittsburgh Pirates. In 2,433 games, he batted .317 with 3,000 hits, 240 home runs, and 1,305 RBI. He was voted the National League's Most Valuable Player (MVP) in 1966, won the World Series MVP in 1971, and was selected to 12 All-Star teams.

mostly used as a defensive replacement for Cassini late in games. Amoros also spent part of the season in Montreal until he was recalled by the Dodgers.

Clemente batted only 148 times for the Royals, hitting just .257 with two home runs and 12 runs batted in (RBI). His batting average was low partly because he was not able to get in a groove and partly because he was so inexperienced that some pitchers made him look foolish. In Stew Thornley's biography on Clemente, Royals manager Max Macon said the youngster "swung wildly." "If you had been in Montreal that year, you wouldn't have believed how ridiculous some pitchers made [Clemente] look," Macon said.

Clemente finally caught a break when he entered the ninth inning of the first game of a doubleheader against Havana on July 25. Clemente hit a home run to win the game in the tenth inning, and Macon rewarded him with a start in the second game of the doubleheader. Over the final seven weeks of the season, Clemente, a right-handed hitter, started every game against left-handed pitchers. He had a few more highlights, including a game-winning home run against Syracuse in August. He also helped the Royals win a game with his powerful arm, throwing a runner out at the plate to preserve an 8-7 victory.

SPANISH OR ENGLISH?

Limited playing time made it a difficult adjustment for Clemente on the field. Language barriers and racial segregation made it even tougher for him off the field. How much English he spoke when he was with Montreal has remained a debatable point through the years. In his book, *Roberto Clemente: The Great One,* author Bruce Markusen quotes two of Clemente's former teammates, each having a different opinion about Roberto's English-speaking skills.

Hall of Fame manager Tommy Lasorda, one of the pitchers on the Royals' staff in 1954, said Clemente only spoke Spanish. "I had to take care of him because he couldn't speak

Branch Rickey *(seated at left)* was the president and general manager of the Brooklyn Dodgers who signed Jackie Robinson, Major League Baseball's first black player, to a contract. Here, in August 1945, Robinson signs a minor league contract as Rickey looks on. Two years later, Robinson appeared in his first major league game. Several years later, Rickey drafted and signed Roberto Clemente to a contract with the Pirates.

one word of English," Lasorda told Phoenix Communications in 1993, according to Markusen. "He couldn't go get anything to eat. So he would wait for me in the morning until I woke up. And then, when I would come down to the lobby, he would be sitting there waiting for me. He was hungry. And I would have to take him to the restaurant and order his meals for him."

Joe Black, another of the Royals' pitchers, and one who would go on to stardom with the Brooklyn Dodgers, said Clemente spoke English. "Puerto Rico, you know, is part of the United States. So, over there, youngsters have the privilege of taking English in classrooms," he said in Markusen's book. "He wouldn't give a speech like Shakespeare, but he knew how to order breakfast and eggs. He knew how to say 'it's a good day,' 'let's play' or 'why I don't play.' He could say 'Let's go to the movies.'" Black contended that Clemente would selectively choose when he wanted to speak English. "He could communicate with those he wanted to communicate with," he said. One thing is clear, however: Clemente did not speak French in Montreal.

LOSING THE GAMBLE

Despite a mediocre first season with the Royals, Clemente showed enough potential that it became apparent to Bavasi the Dodgers would lose him in the postseason draft. Bavasi turned to Pirates president Branch Rickey, who had signed barrier breaker Jackie Robinson when he was the Dodgers' president. Since Pittsburgh had the first pick in the draft, Bavasi wanted to convince Rickey to select another player from the Royals because each team could lose only one player.

Bavasi had a solid working relationship with Rickey from their days together with the Dodgers, and he arranged for the Pirates to take pitcher John Rutherford from the Royals. The deal fell through, however, because Rickey got into an argument with Dodgers' owner Walter O'Malley, according to Thornley. On November, 22, 1954, the Pirates chose Clemente as the first overall pick in the postseason draft.

"I didn't even know where Pittsburgh was," Clemente later confessed. Nevertheless, Clemente joined the Pirates, eager to embark on a career that would eventually earn him a place in baseball's Hall of Fame.

Carolina Kid

Americans love rags to riches stories: real-life tales of men and women born into poverty who rise to success due to sheer determination and effort. The story of Roberto Clemente, baseball superstar, is one of these legends, with a twist: Once he rose to stardom, Clemente never forgot his less-than-glamorous origins.

Puerto Rico, an island in the Caribbean Sea off the coast of Florida, has been a territory of the United States since 1898. Before then, Puerto Rico had been a Spanish colony since 1493, when Christopher Columbus first landed there and claimed it for Spain. It was a valuable asset, since it exported goods such as coffee and sugar (the latter would become the more profitable of the two exports). Unfortunately, Puerto Rico also became a hub of the Atlantic slave trade.

When Columbus arrived in Puerto Rico, he found it populated mostly by Native American tribes, specifically Taino Indians. These tribes were quickly enslaved and forced to mine for gold, which Columbus and his crew were eager to find. Soon, Africans were brought to the island, and their numbers steadily rose as the slave trade increased. The population of the island became mixed—part Indian, part African, and part white. That racial diversity of the island continues to be one of its main features today. Slavery was finally abolished in Puerto Rico in 1873.

In 1898, after it defeated Spain in the Spanish-American War, the United States assumed control of Puerto Rico and claimed it as an American territory. Although Puerto Rico was not, and is still not, a U.S. state, Puerto Ricans are American citizens.

Sugar was the lifeblood of the Puerto Rican economy and had been since the 1500s. Many Puerto Ricans were employed on the island's sugarcane farms, planting and harvesting the crop that kept the economy alive.

One of these men was Melchor Clemente, who lived in Carolina, southeast of the island's capital city of San Juan. Born in the late 1800s, when Puerto Rico was still a Spanish colony, Melchor worked as a foreman for one of the largest sugarcane companies on the island, Central Victoria. Although he was not rich, Melchor was able to provide his family certain comforts that others could not afford, such as a solid roof over their heads, daily meals, and even electricity.

Melchor's own family were poor sugarcane workers of African and Taino Indian ancestry. Like many others in Puerto Rico, Melchor had dark skin. Although racism occurs in Puerto Rico, where citizens are varied in terms of the shade of their skin color, it was not so severe an issue as some Puerto Ricans experienced when arriving in the United States. Roberto Clemente, for example, would experience

For hundreds of years, planting and harvesting sugar fueled the economy of Puerto Rico. Many sugarcane workers lived in poverty in small shacks on the plantations. Roberto Clemente's father, Melchor, came from a poor family that worked the plantations, but he rose to become a foreman for a sugarcane company.

racism more severe than he ever had experienced when he began playing baseball on the U.S. mainland.

Melchor married Luisa Walker Oquendo, a young widow who already had two children. Like her husband, Luisa also had dark skin. Clemente biographer David Maraniss notes that "Luisa's family, the Walkers, came from Loiza, the next town east from Carolina and the nave of blackness on the island. Runaway slaves, known as *cimarrones*, hid from the Spanish Army there in the dense, tangled mangrove swamps off the Atlantic Coast, and formed their own community."[1] Luisa and Melchor had four children together, three boys and a daughter, when Roberto was born on August 18, 1934.

Maraniss relates a popular story about the birth of this baby. The youngest child, Anairis, told her pregnant mother, Luisa, that she wished her new sibling would be a boy and that he would have white skin. When Roberto Clemente Walker was finally presented to his older sister, she was told, "Here he is—a little dark."[2]

While Melchor Clemente did well as a foreman for the Central Victoria sugarcane company, his salary still amounted to less than $50 a month. That amount had to stretch to feed and provide clothing for five children, two stepchildren, and an assortment of cousins and other family members who lived with the family. The Clemente house was a wooden structure with five rooms, including a kitchen, one bathroom, and a living room, so sleeping arrangements were usually very crowded. Furthermore, many of the sugarcane workers stopped by from the nearby field for their meals, so the Clemente house was always filled to capacity with people.

Melchor's salary often had to be supplemented. The entire family helped out. Melchor owned a truck that he used to earn extra money by hauling equipment or assorted items for other people. Luisa sewed at home for further income and also operated a small grocery store out of the house on weekends, according to Maraniss. She also cooked and made lunches for the sugarcane workers. Like many Puerto Rican women, she was not afraid of hard work and labored side-by-side with her husband to provide for their family. Even the children worked, carrying pails of water and ice to the workers in the field to earn a few cents.

One example is a perfect illustration of how scarce money was for the Clemente family. When he was nine years old,

(continues on page 18)

LATINO PRIDE

Since he first entered the major leagues, Roberto Clemente specifically referred to himself as a Puerto Rican player. Although the first Latin-American player, Luis Castro of Colombia, had entered the major leagues as early as 1902, the presence of Latin-American players in professional baseball had not yet reached its peak. Latin-American athletes were still a rarity in American professional sports. Furthermore, Latino players faced discrimination, especially those like Roberto Clemente, who had dark skin.

Clemente tried to educate people about Puerto Rico because he was fiercely proud of his Puerto Rican heritage, but he knew that the country was misunderstood by many Americans. In fact, many Americans did not even know that Puerto Rico was an American territory, and therefore, Puerto Ricans are American citizens, and not "foreigners."

Clemente also did not like the way that some Americans tried to change his identity in subtle ways, to make him seem and sound less Hispanic. For example, when he first entered the major leagues, he was commonly called "Bob" Clemente, an Americanized version of his first name, by sportswriters, announcers, and the media in general. He insisted, however, that people refer to and address him as "Roberto." He did not want to change, and instead, he insisted that people accept him for who he was.

The time that Roberto arrived in the United States to play baseball was a turbulent time in American history. Segregation was still legal, and it was lawful to force African Americans and other people of color to separate themselves in all aspects of life, including on buses, in restaurants, and even in hospitals and schools. When he first joined the Pirates, Clemente was outraged by how he was subjected to the Jim Crow laws of the segregated United States. Because of his dark skin, he was considered to be African American by some people and therefore subject to the laws of segregation.

This lifestyle was a shock for Roberto. In Puerto Rico, where people of all shades of skin mingled freely and all levels of society were integrated, he had never experienced feeling different. On the mainland United States, however, he felt like an outsider, especially during away games, when the team traveled to the Southern states. Often he had to stay in separate hotel facilities from his white teammates. Sometimes, when the team bus stopped at a restaurant so the players could eat, he and the other dark-skinned members of the Pirates had to wait on the bus for a white teammate to bring out some food for them because the restaurant's policy was not to serve "Negroes."

For Clemente, playing for the Pirates came with a sense of responsibility: he felt that he had to educate people about both Puerto Rican heritage and the importance of ending segregation and racism. He could do this through his personal example, by being the best player on the field he could possibly be as well as the best human being off the field.

Whenever he could, he remembered to acknowledge his Puerto Rican heritage. The year he won the batting title for the National League, the Sportswriters Fraternity of Puerto Rico sponsored a homecoming party for him and Orlando Cepeda, a fellow Puerto Rican who had captured the home run and RBI titles that year. It was the first time in major league history that Puerto Rican players had secured all three batting titles.

When it was his turn to speak, Clemente spoke in Spanish, which was something he did often for two reasons: He felt more comfortable speaking in his native language, and it served to remind people of his Latin-American heritage. On that occasion, he said, "In the name of my family, in the name of Puerto Rico, in the name of all the players who didn't have a chance to play for Puerto Rico in the big leagues, I thank you. You can be sure that all the Puerto Rican players who go to the States do their best."

(continued from page 15)

young Roberto decided he needed a bicycle. His father could not afford to buy him one, so Roberto began saving pennies he earned from delivering pails of water to the workers in the fields. It took him three years to save up enough to buy the bicycle—he was 12 before he was able to enjoy the fruit of his labor.

Though Roberto Clemente grew up relatively poor, his childhood was generally fulfilling. Carolina was a rural area, as yet untouched by the nearby big city of San Juan, and because the Clemente house was so crowded, Roberto spent a lot of his time playing outdoors. The neighborhood children had miles of fields at their disposal. They played a variety of games and had many adventures, but there was one sport in particular that was king in Carolina, and indeed all over Puerto Rico.

THE KING SPORT

Baseball, a uniquely American sport, had reached Puerto Rico decades before Roberto Clemente's birth. The game was invented in the 1840s by Alexander Joy Cartwright (1820–1892) of New York. Along with the members of his club, the New York Knickerbocker Base Ball Club, Cartwright developed the rules of the game, which are based loosely on the English game of rounders, which dates back to at least the 1700s. When Cartwright published his rules of baseball, the game caught on and became wildly popular. Before long, it was being referred to as "America's favorite pastime."

In Puerto Rico, the sport's popularity was equally intense, and the island eventually played a significant role in the development of American baseball. On the mainland United States, racial segregation was still widespread, and African Americans and other people of color in general were excluded from playing in professional sports, including baseball. These ostracized players often found Puerto Rico to be a receptive and welcoming place, whose fans appreciated their talents and did not care about the color of their skin.

In the 1930s, the Puerto Rican Professional Baseball League was established on the island, drawing professional players from the United States who wanted to earn extra money during the winter break by playing in Puerto Rico's mild climate. Many of these players included African Americans, who were barred from the professional leagues until 1947, when Jackie Robinson made his historic debut with the Brooklyn Dodgers. African-American ballplayers in the United States played in the Negro League, and its many teams traveled the country playing at stadiums and fields everywhere. Some of the Negro League's star players included Josh Gibson, Monte Irvin, Ford Smith, and many others who also traveled every winter to the Caribbean to play.

The color line did not matter in Puerto Rico. African Americans and white baseball players were equally welcome. Puerto Rican fans only cared about watching a good game. Skills, not skin color, determined the player's popularity and the type of reception they received.

It was almost inevitable that Roberto Clemente would get caught up in baseball at a young age. "When I was a little kid," he once said, "the only thing I used to do was play ball all the time . . . with a paper ball, with a rubber ball, with a tennis ball."[3] With whatever they could find or fashion, it did not matter—the game had to go on. Many stories are told about how Clemente had his humble beginnings in the sport, using the branch of a guava tree for a bat and a bunch of rags or tightly wound strings for a ball.

Roberto and the other neighborhood kids closely followed the two main teams that played in the San Juan area, the San Juan Senadores (Senators) and the Santurce Cangrejeros (Crabbers). One of Roberto's heroes was the African-American ballplayer Monte Irvin, an outfielder who played in both the Negro Leagues and the Mexican League and often spent the winter season playing for the Senadores.

Montford Merrill Irvin, an Alabama native who was raised in New Jersey, was born in 1919. Like other African-American

Hard-hitting outfielder Monte Irvin played eight seasons in the major leagues, posting a .293 batting average with 99 home runs and 443 RBI. In 1951, he led the National League with 121 RBI. Irvin did not play in his first major league game until he was 30 years old because of the color barrier, an unwritten "rule" that kept black players out of Major League Baseball.

players before him, Irvin struggled with the reality of possessing a talent that was overlooked in the professional leagues because of his skin color. He made his mark as a powerful batter and competent fielder in the nonprofessional leagues, but when Jackie Robinson finally broke the color line in 1947 and baseball was more willing to sign African-American players, Irvin was quickly signed by the New York Giants in 1949. He played with the Giants for seven seasons and then played one season with the Chicago Cubs. After he retired, he worked as a scout and a public relations officer. Irvin was inducted into the Baseball Hall of Fame in 1973.

When Roberto Clemente was growing up, Monte Irvin was at the peak of his talent. The young Clemente was consistently amazed by Irvin's speed, power, and grace on the playing field, and he wanted to emulate him. Roberto would take the bus to the Sixto Escobar, the stadium where the Cangrejeros and the Senadores both played, to watch Monte Irvin play. Melchor Clemente would often give Roberto the 25 cents he needed for the bus ride and admission to the stadium. Roberto often arrived early to be able to glimpse Irvin enter the field, and he eventually got an opportunity to speak to his idol.

Monte Irvin, who had been voted Most Valuable Player of the Puerto Rican winter leagues, was impressed by the dedication of young Roberto and soon befriended the boy. According to Maraniss, "Irvin made sure that his young fan got in to watch the game, even without a ticket,"[4] often letting Roberto walk in carrying Irvin's bag so he would not have to pay the admittance fee. For young Roberto Clemente, being so close to his sports idol, and having that idol take such a personal interest in him, was invaluable to shaping his future ambitions.

A Big Break

As a teenager, Roberto Clemente quickly became involved with some of Carolina's many youth teams. He played shortstop for a softball team that was coached by Roberto Marin, who had seen him play once with the other neighborhood kids and convinced him to sign up for the team. Marin was instrumental in encouraging Clemente to pursue baseball, and he would eventually become one of Clemente's career mentors. This was an important role to play because Melchor Clemente was too busy working to understand and encourage his youngest son in the sport. In fact, Melchor barely understood how the game was played and considered it just a hobby and not a potential career path for his son. Roberto also played outfield for a hardball team, the Juncos Mules, in Carolina, where he honed his most amazing skills: his powerful throwing arm and quick base running.

By 1952, when Roberto had just turned 18, he was signed to play for the Santurce Cangrejeros, owned by Pedrin Zorilla. Roberto Marin had told Zorilla earlier that Clemente was essentially a star in the making, and after watching Roberto on the field, the Cangrejeros' owner agreed and took Clemente on his squad. During that first season, Clemente was still in high school and was the youngest member of the team. Melchor Clemente was unsure whether he should allow his son to play, questioning whether the teen could build a career and a future for himself by playing the game. Roberto, begged his father to allow him to play for the Cangrejeros, and so Melchor finally consented.

Roberto's salary, $40 a week, as well as a $400 signing bonus, did not seem like much, but it definitely contributed to the family's income, and Roberto felt proud to be able to help, especially since Melchor was already nearly 70 years old by that time. Roberto was keenly aware of the family's difficult circumstances. Whenever he asked his father for a quarter to take the bus to Sixto Escobar stadium, he knew that 25 cents was not an insignificant amount. He was also aware of how much pain the family had experienced. The Clemente family had endured tremendous suffering during Roberto's childhood and adolescence. For one thing, poverty, and the fear of it, always loomed in the background. Tragedy was another: when Roberto was still a baby, his sister Anairis died when her clothing caught on fire. While she was playing near the large outdoor oven that Luisa used to cook meals for Melchor's workers, gasoline spilled on the flames and ignited the little girl's dress, causing serious burns on over 90 percent of her body. She died in the hospital a few days later, after suffering tremendous pain. The family was devastated and haunted by her horrible death.

Roberto learned the value of hard work, often spending his time after school running errands and performing chores to earn a few pennies whenever he could. His schoolwork also

Clemente signed with the Santurce Cangrejeros of the Puerto Rican winter league when he was 18 years old. Still going strong today, the winter league gives professional baseball players an opportunity to play ball during the major league off-season months. Other Major League Baseball stars who played in the league include Willie Mays, Bernie Williams, Cal Ripken Jr., and Rickey Henderson.

proved to be difficult. At the Julio Vizcarrando High School, lessons were taught in English, and Roberto, who spoke only Spanish, struggled to keep up with the pace of the curriculum and his classmates. One of his teachers, the wife of Roberto Marin, noticed that Roberto had a hard time academically, and she went out of her way to help him. "Despite his shyness," she said, "and the sadness around his eyes, there was something poignantly appealing about him."[5]

Indeed, despite his boundless energy on the field, Roberto was actually a deeply thoughtful and introspective person. He was considerate and took his time. Whenever anyone interrupted his thoughts or his actions, his response was *"momentito,"* which he repeated so often that the family began to call him "Momen," a name that would stick to him for the rest of his life.

Baseball was Roberto's escape. While he also became interested in track and field in high school, excelling at the javelin throw, he still played baseball during every spare moment. It is not certain whether he ever imagined that baseball would be his future career, but when he was signed by the Cangrejeros and suddenly earning a respectable salary, the future seemed to arrive more quickly than anyone could have thought.

THOSE WHO CAME BEFORE

One wonders if Clemente ever imagined himself playing in the major leagues, or whether he saw this goal as too daunting and not something he could achieve because of the many obstacles in the way. Sometimes, people refer to Clemente as the first Latino player to star in the professional baseball leagues. This is actually not true. Latinos had played for years before Clemente made the journey to the United States mainland. The difference was that these Latinos often had light skin and passed as white players.

The first Puerto Rican to play in the American major leagues was Hiram Bithorn, a talented pitcher who was well known as a hero to Clemente and his friends. Born in 1916, Bithorn hailed from Santurce, not far from Carolina, where Clemente grew up. He played for the Senadores and had a spectacular career. The Chicago Cubs signed him as a pitcher in 1942, five years before Jackie Robinson integrated baseball. He spent some time in the United States military during World War II, but when he returned to baseball, his talent seemed to be defused. He had a tough time recouping his former glory, and his life ended tragically in Mexico, when he was shot and fatally wounded by a Mexican police officer. Nobody really knows the circumstances of the shooting, but his death at the age of 35 cemented Bithorn's status as a legend for his Puerto Rican fans.

Vic Power was another Latino who broke the barrier by playing in the United States major leagues. Born Victor Felipe Pellot Pove in 1927, he was signed by the New York Yankees in 1951, although he never started a game for the team. It was not until 1954, when he finally was signed by the Philadelphia Athletics, that Victor, now known as Vic Power—the Pove having been changed to Power—became the first Puerto Rican to play in the American League. As a dark-skinned Latino, this was an even more significant achievement because of the intensity of the racial discrimination he faced. After all, baseball had been integrated for less than a decade by that point.

However, Power handled the discrimination with a sarcastic sense of humor and wit. Once, while eating in a restaurant, he was told by the waitress that they did not serve Negroes. He quickly replied, "That's okay . . . I don't eat Negroes." His witty style quickly became one of his trademarks, as did his outstanding performance on the field. In his 12-year career, Power was selected to four American League All-Star teams, and he won seven consecutive Gold Glove Awards (1958–1964) for his flashy fielding skills at first base.

Legends like Bithorn and Power certainly influenced young, soon-to-be stars like Clemente. Players such as these proved that Puerto Ricans could be recruited and could have tremendous success playing for the professional leagues in the United States.

In his major league career, Roberto Clemente batted over .300 13 times. He led National League hitters in 1961 (.351), 1964 (.339), 1965 (.329), and 1967 (.357). He also led the league in hits in 1964 with 211 and in 1967 with 209. Here, Clemente bats against the Chicago Cubs in a game played in 1965.

THE DODGERS

While playing for the Cangrejeros, Roberto attended a tryout that the Brooklyn Dodgers were holding, in November 1952, at Sixto Escobar Stadium near San Juan. Al Campanis, an

(continues on page 30)

A TRIO OF SUPPORT

It was Roberto Marin who first recognized Roberto Clemente's skill as a baseball player. Marin had watched young Roberto playing in the streets of Carolina with his friends and knew that, with some practice and polishing, the handsome young boy could one day become a star.

Clemente never forgot Marin and always remained sentimental about how Marin had helped him and encouraged him to pursue baseball as a career. Whenever he had a chance, he acknowledged Marin as a coach and a mentor. Marin's support was especially important because it came so early in Clemente's career, when he was still a young boy. Clemente felt that his own father, Melchor, did not completely understand his zeal and enthusiasm for baseball. Melchor, a hardworking man, felt that sports was a hobby and would not result in a career for his son, although he was happy that playing gave Roberto pleasure. (In fact, Melchor hardly understood the sport or its rules. He once watched his son play and commented that he felt sorry for him: it seemed senseless to the practical Melchor that Roberto should spend his time running around the bases and wearing himself out!) It was Marin who could sense Roberto's desire to pursue baseball as a career, so his encouragement was vital.

Pedrin Zorrilla, nicknamed the "Big Crab," was another mentor of Clemente's. The original owner of the Santurce Cangrejeros who had signed Clemente when he was still in high school, Zorrilla followed Clemente's career closely and provided him encouragement and support. It was easy for the Big Crab to see that Clemente possessed a special talent for baseball and that he would one day be a superb player, though it is uncertain whether even Zorrilla knew Clemente would become an American legend one day. Yet, he did do everything he could to help Clemente get into the American professional leagues. Zorrilla, who was also a scout for the Brooklyn Dodgers and other teams, was Clemente's main connection to getting a major league contract.

Clemente never forgot his debts. After the 1968 season, he finally took a much-needed break from playing in the Puerto Rican League during the winter season. He planned to do the same during the 1969 winter break because he wanted to spend time with his growing family as well as to give his body a rest. Yet, when the Big Crab called and asked for a personal favor, Clemente did not turn him down.

Zorrilla was by then the general manager for the San Juan Senadores, and he wanted Clemente on his team's roster. He knew Roberto planned on a break, but thought he would ask anyway.

"Don Pedro, whatever you say, I will play," replied Roberto dutifully.[*] He did not even ask what his salary would be. He knew that the man who had helped him reach stardom as a major league player would treat him fairly when it came to getting paid.

A third close confidante of Roberto was someone he could talk to about things other than his baseball career: his wife, Vera. Roberto admired the self-possessed way she conducted herself and he respected her opinion. Vera shared his passion for helping people, and she supported his many efforts to draw attention to the plight of the poor in Latin American countries. In fact, in 1972, she encouraged him to undergo a humanitarian mission to Nicaragua, where an earthquake had ravaged the nation. She was proud of Roberto for using his fame as a baseball player to better the lives of other people in the world, especially those who were the most vulnerable, such as children. After his death, Vera continued to preserve his vision, especially by pursuing many charitable causes in his memory and his honor.

[*] Quoted in David Maraniss, *Clemente: The Passion and Grace of Baseball's Last Hero* (New York: Simon and Schuster, 2006), 233.

(continued from page 27)

important and influential scout for Brooklyn, was watching the players on the field when he noticed the young, handsome Clemente. Campanis was impressed by Clemente's skills. According to Maraniss's biography, after seeing Clemente's top-notch fielding abilities, Campanis was bowled over. If Clemente was even a somewhat decent batter, he would be happy, saying, "If the sonofagun can hold a bat in his hands, I'm gonna sign the guy."[6]

Clemente could indeed hold a bat in his hands. He could swing it too, very hard and very skillfully. In his scouting report, Campanis noted, "Will mature into big man. Attending high school but plays with Santurce. Has all the tools and likes to play. A real good-looking prospect!"[7] He also noted that Clemente was a "definite prospect."

Shortly after he finished high school, Clemente was courted by five major league teams: the Milwaukee Braves, the Dodgers, the St. Louis Cardinals, the Boston Red Sox, and the Giants. Clemente wanted to play in New York because of the large Puerto Rican community there, so the Giants and Dodgers were the only serious contenders to sign him. The Dodgers won out in the end because they offered a better deal: $5,000 salary and a $10,000 signing bonus. Although top white prospects were offered much more money than that to sign, Clemente agreed. His father, Melchor, signed the contract on his behalf.[8]

The Dodgers felt Clemente was not ready for the major leagues right away, so they sent him to their minor league club in Montreal to help him adjust to his new situation and polish his skills. The media, meanwhile, announced that Brooklyn had signed a new "Negro player" to its minor league team. This was just the beginning of the issues of race that were to challenge Clemente. Though he considered himself Puerto Rican, in the United States during the 1950s, Clemente was considered a Negro because of the dark color of his skin, and he would face prejudice unlike anything else he had experienced thus far in his life. Dealing with American segregation was startling for someone who had grown up in an environment where people of different skin shades coexisted peacefully. Seeing African Americans relegated to the back of public buses and banned from certain restaurants was a shock for young Roberto.

Furthermore, although he was excited to be playing in the United States, Clemente soon became frustrated in a Royals uniform. In reality, he was the only Puerto Rican on the Royals as well as the team's youngest player, but the real problem was that he hardly had a chance to play.

Though he had made an excellent debut in his first few games, Roberto was soon taken off the starting roster. He appeared in very few games, although he wanted nothing more than to play and show his abilities on the field. One theory for the Dodgers' strange welcoming of Clemente is that the team wanted to hide Clemente, in case another team realized his worth and tried to trade him. Bob Watt, an employee of the Royals at the time, acknowledged that the team wanted to keep Clemente's talent a secret: "Whenever we'd spot a scout in the stands, that would be the end of Clemente for that day. He never had the chance to show what he could do."[9]

As much as he had wanted to go to the United States mainland and play for a major league team, Clemente now wished he could go elsewhere. All he wanted to do was play ball.

4

Where Is Pittsburgh?

Roberto Clemente was playing with future Hall of Famer Willie Mays for the Santurce Cangrejeros in Puerto Rico when he heard the news that would change his life and have a dramatic affect on his baseball career. It was November 22, 1954, and Major League Baseball was holding its annual postseason draft. Dodgers' vice president Buzzie Bavasi desperately wanted to keep Clemente in the organization. Clemente spent the season with Brooklyn's Triple-A minor league team in Montreal because the Dodgers claimed that they had no room for him on the big league roster. All-stars Carl Furillo, Duke Snider, and Jackie Robinson held the outfield spots with the Dodgers.

Bavasi tried to arrange it so that the Pittsburgh Pirates, who had the first overall pick because they had the worst record in the league, would select another Dodgers player. Each team could only lose one player, so Bavasi knew he could keep Clemente if the Pirates took someone else.

Historian Stew Thornley wrote that Bavasi turned to Branch Rickey, who ran the Dodgers before going to Pittsburgh. Rickey wanted Bavasi to join him in the Pirates' front office, but Bavasi declined the offer. Still, Rickey told Bavasi to call him if he ever needed a favor. Bavasi sure needed one right now.

Bavasi arranged for Rickey to agree to draft pitcher John Rutherford from the Montreal Royals. Two days later, however, Bavasi learned the deal was off because Dodgers owner Walter O'Malley got into an argument with Rickey. "It seems Walter called Mr. Rickey every name in the book," Bavasi told Thornley. "Thus, we lost Roberto."

The Dodgers gambled they could hide Clemente in the minors, but his enormous potential was clear to the scouts that saw him play, even if it was just a few times. After a frustrating season with Montreal, Clemente was thrilled he was going to a team that would give him an opportunity to play regularly. He was eager to show the fans he could play.

There was only one question on Clemente's mind: "Where is Pittsburgh?" he said, according to Paul Robert Walker's biography, *Pride of Puerto Rico.*

A TOUGH WINTER

An outfield of Clemente, Mays, and Bob Thurman gave Santurce probably the best trio ever in the Puerto Rican League. Mays already had established himself as a star player in the major leagues, helping the New York Giants win the 1951 World Series and earning the National League Most Valuable Player Award that season. Clemente and Mays provided several highlights for Santurce fans and each player hit a home run in the league's All-Star game.

Off the field, Clemente and his family had to deal with a sad tragedy. One of his brothers, Luis Oquendo, Luisa's son from her first marriage, was diagnosed with a brain tumor. A schoolteacher in Puerto Rico, Luis had been suffering for many months with headaches and seizures. By the time the

In 1954, Clemente played with Willie Mays *(swinging)* for the Santurce Cangrejeros, the team that won the Puerto Rican winter league championship that season. Mays, considered by many baseball experts to be the greatest player who ever lived, played 22 seasons in the majors, hitting a lifetime .302 with 660 home runs and 1,903 RBI. Here, in a game played in 1970, Willie connects with the 3,000th hit of his career.

brain tumor was diagnosed, it was too late for him to have a chance to survive. Roberto visited his brother at the hospital throughout his illness.

Shortly after Christmas 1954, Luis underwent brain surgery to have the tumor removed and to determine whether it was malignant or benign, that is, to see if it was cancerous or not. Roberto and two of his other brothers drove late at night to make it to the hospital to be with Luis. Roberto was driving the vehicle when a drunk driver ran through a red light and crashed into the car. His brothers were unharmed, but

Roberto hurt his neck and spine. Though he insisted he was fine, the accident damaged some of Clemente's spinal discs, which would plague him for the rest of his career. When they finally got to the hospital, it was only to learn the worst of possible news: Luis's tumor was indeed malignant. There was nothing that could be done for him. On December 31, 1954, Luis died. He was only 38 years old.

Even though it was difficult, Clemente knew he had to continue playing baseball to help take his mind off the tragedy. Santurce finished in first place and advanced to the playoffs. With Mays and Clemente leading the way, Santurce captured its second Caribbean Series championship in three years.

Now it was time for Clemente to make his mark in the major leagues. The Pirates carefully watched Clemente during the winter and knew he could be special with hard work and dedication. "He can run, throw and hit. He needs much polishing, though, because he is a rough diamond," Rickey said in a *Sporting News* article on February 9, 1955.

MAKING THE TEAM

Clemente went to spring training with the Pirates in Florida in 1955 hoping to earn a spot on the roster. Pittsburgh had finished in last place three straight years, but they still had an abundance of outfield talent. Roberto had plenty of competition for a spot.

When the Pirates' best outfielder, Frank Thomas, sat out the first part of spring training because he wanted more money, Clemente seized the opportunity to showcase his skills. Clemente impressed manager Fred Haney with his tools and, perhaps more importantly, his willingness to take instruction and the ability to apply it and learn from mistakes. "The boy has the tools, there's no doubt about that. And he takes to instruction readily. Certainly I have been pleased with what I have seen," Haney said in a *Sporting News* article on March 16, 1955. "He has some faults, which were expected, but let's wait and see." When Thomas resolved his salary dispute and finally reported to camp, he got sick and missed more time, opening the door for Clemente to make the team and head north to Pittsburgh with the Pirates.

Once Clemente arrived in Pittsburgh and saw how big and spacious Forbes Field was, he knew it would not be easy to hit a lot of home runs. The Pirates had played in Forbes Field since 1909. It was the biggest park in the league, with a distance of 365 feet (111 meters) down the left-field line and 457 feet (139 meters) to the power alley in left-center field.

THE HISTORY OF THE BUCS

When Roberto Clemente first heard that he had been traded to the Pirates, he did not even know where Pittsburgh was, yet he would spend the rest of his professional baseball career playing for this team.

Originally known as the Pittsburgh Alleghenies, because of Pittsburgh's proximity to the Allegheny Mountains (or as others contend, because of the Allegheny River, one of three rivers that runs through the city), the ball club was founded in 1887, making it one of Major League Baseball's oldest clubs. They were renamed the Pirates in December 1891, at the close of the season. By this time, the National League had been formed, and the Pirates—known as the Bucs—were part of its central division. The origin of the team nickname came about when Lou Bierbauer, a second baseman for the Philadelphia Athletics, found himself the center of controversy. As play-ers were reassigned to the different leagues, he was sent to Pittsburgh because of a technicality (the Athletics had not reserved him to remain on its team during the reassigning of leagues), and so Pittsburgh's team was referred to as "pirates" for stealing him away.

The Pirates earned their first World Series title in 1907, having defeated the Detroit Tigers. They did not win another

Clemente figured he could take advantage of the space in the gaps by hitting line drives and using his speed to get doubles and triples.

Interestingly, the Pirates listed his name as "Bob" because Roberto sounded too foreign. Though he weighed only 175 pounds, Clemente used a 36-ounce bat, heavier than most sluggers. A right-handed hitter, Clemente stood far off the plate, spread his legs wide, held his bat high and took a long stride toward the plate when he swung. He had quick hands

series again until 1925, when they defeated the Washington Senators. The next quarter century was not a good era in the history of the Pirates, whose winning record was shaky, to say the least. Yet things began to change in 1950 when James Galbreath, a real estate tycoon, became the team's owner.

Over the next several years, the Pirates got rid of the well-paid older players and drafted several young talents. The new general manager, hired by Galbreath, was Branch Rickey, who had integrated baseball by signing Jackie Robinson to play for the Brooklyn Dodgers in 1947. Rickey was also the inventor of the farm system, in which a major league team has a parallel minor league team that helps provide new, young players with more experience before they move up to the big leagues.

By 1960, the team was solid and much more stable (it included Roberto Clemente by then), which was evident when the Bucs defeated the New York Yankees to win the World Series. They would win two more Series, in 1971 and 1979.

The death of Roberto Clemente in 1972 was a major professional and personal loss to the Pirates and their fans. The city of Pittsburgh has remembered him by naming a bridge and a park near PNC Stadium after Clemente, as well as erecting a statue in his honor.

and strong arms, making it easier to drive outside pitches to right field.

Clemente did not appear in the starting lineup for the Pirates' first three games of the season, but he got his chance in the first game of a doubleheader on Sunday, April 17, 1955. Ironically, the Pirates' opponent for Clemente's major league debut was the Brooklyn Dodgers. The excitement began building for Clemente the moment he saw his name on the lineup card. Not only did he want to prove himself before the home crowd, he wanted to show the Dodgers they were wrong to let him go.

Clemente's first at bat came against left-hander Johnny Podres. With two outs in the bottom of the first inning, Clemente singled off shortstop Pee Wee Reese's glove for his first major league hit.

He also started the second game of the doubleheader, getting a single and double. Clemente hit his first home run, an inside-the-park shot, in the following game, against the New York Giants. For the next three weeks, the rookie was on fire, making himself a difficult out for opposing pitchers. Clemente led the Pirates in batting with a .360 average three weeks into the season. His exceptional speed on the base paths drew raves, and his standout play on defense, especially his powerful throwing arm, made him a fan favorite.

Still, Clemente had some problems adjusting to a new city and new teammates. Some players had not accepted blacks playing in the major leagues, even though Jackie Robinson broke the color barrier in 1947. Hearing insults infuriated Clemente, who was not used to such despicable treatment in Puerto Rico. Writers also were hard on Clemente. Some exaggerated his accent in newspaper quotes. One writer even called him a "Puerto Rican hot dog."

The back injury Clemente suffered in the car accident the previous winter caused him a lot of pain and forced him to sit out some games. That made it worse because some writers and players accused Clemente of "jaking it," baseball slang for pretending to be hurt. Doctors said there was nothing wrong with his back, but Clemente would get sore whenever he played too many games in a row. The accusations that he was faking the pain bothered Clemente because ever since he was a small boy playing in Puerto Rico, he badly wanted to play baseball. He could not understand why anyone would think he pretended to be hurt.

As his rookie season wore on, Clemente slumped at the plate because he had trouble staying away from bad pitches. His frustration was clear each time he angrily broke a batting helmet. At one point, Pirates manager Fred Haney threatened to fine Clemente for each broken helmet after the total reached 22.

"I don't mind you tearing up your own clothes," Haney said in Walker's *Pride of Puerto Rico*. "But if you're going to destroy club property, you're going to pay for it." Told the cost of each helmet was $10, Clemente quickly did the math and decided he could not afford to pay for them so he had to curb his temper. "OK, I stop breaking the hats," he replied.

Clemente finished his rookie season with a respectable .255 batting average, five homers, 11 triples, 23 doubles, and 47 RBI in 124 games and 474 at bats. His lack of patience at the plate was evident by the fact that he drew just 18 walks. Clemente was not a rookie sensation, but he proved he belonged in the big leagues, and fans were excited to see more of the young ballplayer.

QUITTING SO SOON

When Clemente returned home to Puerto Rico following his rookie year, he was not sure whether he wanted to go back to Pittsburgh the following season. The thought of being traded by the Pirates was not the reason, though. Rather, he was considering quitting baseball because he had a lot of pain in his back, and he was disappointed with the way his first year went in Pittsburgh. It upset him a great deal that some people thought he was faking an injury just so he did not have to play.

The media had already started to call him a "hypochondriac," or a person who imagines he is constantly ill. He knew he had not shown Pittsburgh fans his best and thought there was no point in playing if he was unable to play at a higher level.

One night at home, Clemente was sitting at the dinner table with his parents. They had a long conversation that helped convince Clemente to stick it out and play for the Pirates another year. His mother thought it would be a good idea for Roberto to go back to school and take classes rather than play for Santurce in the winter league, but he decided to continuing playing.

"Mama, baseball is my life," Clemente said, according to Walker's *Pride of Puerto Rico.* Clemente's father told him he had to make the decision on his own because he was a man now. "I will try it one more year. If I still hurt, then I [will] quit," Clemente said.

THE NEW-LOOK PIRATES

While Clemente was thinking about his baseball future, the Pirates were making sweeping changes. Branch Rickey retired as general manager to become team president. New general manager, Joe L. Brown, hired Bobby Bragan to replace Fred Haney as the manager. Players liked Bragan's personality, but he also showed a strict side.

Early in the season, Clemente missed a bunt sign during a game. He did not miss the sign on purpose, but still he failed to execute the bunt. Bragan fined him $25. Bragan also fined another player, Dale Long, for a different infraction. This let Clemente know he was not being singled out by the new manager.

By May, the Pirates had acquired talented center fielder Bill Virdon in a trade. They also called up second baseman Bill Mazeroski from the minors. This gave Pittsburgh a solid mix of players with Clemente in right field, Long at first base, Frank Thomas at third base, and Dick Groat playing shortstop. This young mix of players invigorated the team with their passion

In this rare series of photos, Roberto Clemente makes a sensational, sprawling catch against the Chicago Cubs in a game played at Chicago's Wrigley Field in 1958. Clemente earned 12 Gold Glove Awards for his outstanding defensive play in right field.

and enthusiasm, and the results showed on the field. By June 13, the Pirates were in first place in the National League, after four consecutive last-place finishes. Yet an eight-game losing streak soon followed, and the Pirates suddenly looked like the same old losing Pirates.

Win or lose, Clemente gave the fans a reason to cheer every time they came to the park. He displayed his strong arm by consistently throwing runners out from right field, and he only missed seven games that season, a sign that his back was feeling better. At the plate, Clemente batted .311, a 56-point increase from his rookie season. One of his biggest hits that season came against the Chicago Cubs in late July.

The Pirates trailed the Cubs 8-5 in the bottom of the ninth inning. The bases were loaded with no outs when Clemente stepped into the batter's box. The Cubs made a pitching change to bring in hard-throwing right-hander Jim Brosnan to face Clemente. Brosnan's first pitch was right down the middle. Clemente slammed it to deep left-center field. All three runners raced around the bases to score the tying runs. Clemente sped around second base and headed for third. Bragan was coaching third base that day, and he threw his hands up for Clemente to stop. There was no sense in sending Clemente home with nobody out because the Pirates only needed a sacrifice fly from either of the next two batters to win the game.

Clemente, however, was not going to wait for another batter to bring him home. He ignored Bragan's stop sign and kept running around third base. The throw to the plate was on line, but Clemente slid underneath the catcher's tag for an inside-the-park grand slam homer that gave the Pirates a 9-8 victory. Bragan was not happy. Although Clemente had showed tremendous base-running skills, he had disobeyed his coach's stop sign at third base. Yet this time Bragan did not issue a fine to his talented sophomore.

Overall, the Pirates showed improvement in Clemente's second season and finished out of last place for the first time since 1951, placing seventh in the National League. (At that time, there were only eight teams in each major league.) Clemente received a large raise in salary after the season, using some of the money to buy a new home for his parents.

5

At a Crossroads

In 1956, Roberto Clemente was leading the Puerto Rican League in batting and had an 18-game hitting streak when new Santurce owner, Pedrin Zorrilla, sold the team, and the new owner made an extremely unpopular decision to trade his star player and other players to the Caguas-Rio Piedras. The move caused Santurce manager, Monchile Concepcion, to resign, and fans were not happy to see Clemente go somewhere else. Yet Clemente kept on hitting, his streak reaching 23 games, to set a new league record. He finished the season with a .396 batting average, but his back problems started to flare up, and he reported to Pirates' spring training a day late in 1957.

Bragan was not too concerned about Clemente's back because he had played so well the previous season through all the aches and pains. "The case history of Clemente is the worse he feels, the better he plays," Bragan said, as reported in *The*

Sporting News on March 13, 1957. "I'd rather have a Clemente with some ailment than a Clemente who says he feels great with no aches or pains."

The back problems were so severe that Clemente needed to wear a back brace throughout the entire season. He played in just 111 games, missing 43 (at the time, major league teams played 154 games each season, rather than the 162-game schedule played today), and his batting average dropped significantly to .253 with only four homers and 30 RBI.

With Clemente struggling, the Pirates had a tough time winning games. Bragan was fired in August and replaced by Danny Murtaugh, a former second baseman with the Pirates who demanded a lot from his players. Under Murtaugh, the Pirates played better the rest of the season but still finished last in the National League. Clemente's back problems lingered throughout the winter, and he did not play in the Puerto Rican League until the middle of January 1958.

A NEW UNIFORM

By the time spring training arrived, Clemente felt much better physically. He was ready to help the Pirates take a tremendous leap in the National League standings. In the season opener, Clemente had three hits against Milwaukee. It was a sign of more to come. He hit a game-winning homer off fellow Puerto Rican Juan Pizarro against Milwaukee on August 4. He also tied a National League record with three triples in a victory over Cincinnati on September 8.

Clemente finished the season with a .289 average, six homers, 10 triples, 50 RBI, and 22 assists from the outfield. His performance helped the Pirates climb from last place to second place, only eight games behind the Braves. The strong season led to high hopes. Many expected the Pirates to contend for the pennant in 1959.

Instead of playing in the Puerto Rican League after the season as he did each winter, Clemente wore a different uniform, this one for the United States Marine Reserves. He

Danny Murtaugh managed the Pittsburgh Pirates for 15 seasons (1957–1964, 1967, 1970–1971, and 1973-1976). As a manager, he compiled a 1,115–960 lifetime record. Before becoming a manager, Murtaugh was a National League second baseman, playing for the Philadelphia Phillies, the Boston Braves, and the Pittsburgh Pirates from 1941–1951.

fulfilled a six-month military commitment at Parris Island, South Carolina, and Camp LeJeune, North Carolina. The rigorous training helped Clemente's back improve, and he added strength by gaining 10 pounds.

None of it mattered, though, because he injured his elbow in May 1959 and had to spend 40 days on the disabled list. Missing games was frustrating for Clemente because he loved to play. It was even more upsetting because some people again began questioning his pain tolerance and whether he was faking his injury. Murtaugh, a tough Irishman, believed his players should play hurt. "You're faking the injury," Murtaugh shouted at Clemente in the dugout one day, according to Walker's *Pride of Puerto Rico.* Murtaugh continued: "Take off the uniform." An angry Clemente replied: "No one takes off my uniform while I am playing for the Pirates."

Clemente batted .296 in only 105 games in 1959. After five seasons in the major leagues, his career batting average was .282. He averaged five homers, 47 RBI, 22 doubles, and eight triples per season. He had just one season with an average above .300 and only once had more than 50 RBI. These were solid numbers, but they certainly did not place Clemente among the elite players in the game such as Mays, Hank Aaron, Mickey Mantle, or Ernie Banks.

When he returned to Puerto Rico following the 1959 season, Clemente thought about his career and what he needed to do to become a great player, not just for himself, but for all the people of Puerto Rico. He elected to play winter ball again, and in 1959–1960 he played a full season in the Puerto Rican League for the first time in several years. He batted .330 for his new team, the San Juan Senadores, and was eager to carry his success over to the Pirates.

BREAKING OUT

Finally free of injuries, Clemente got off to a great start in 1960. He batted .386 in April, and the Pirates finished the month off with eight straight wins. Clemente stayed hot, even when the Pirates cooled off in May. He had 25 RBI in 27 games that month, raising his season total to 39. He helped the Pirates to first place, and they continued to battle the San Francisco Giants and Milwaukee Braves for the league lead the rest of the summer.

In early August, Clemente injured his knee and cut his shin while making an outstanding catch on a drive by his former Santurce teammate, Willie Mays. The Pirates held on to beat the Giants 1-0, but Clemente missed a week of action following the mishap. Pittsburgh's lead in the standings dropped from seven games to two games without Clemente in the lineup.

On Clemente's second day back, he drove in all four runs in a 4-1 win over the St. Louis Cardinals. The Pirates then swept a doubleheader against the Cardinals the next day and never looked back. Led by Clemente, shortstop Dick Groat, and pitchers Vernon Law and Bob Friend, they won the National League pennant by seven games over the Braves, topping the league for the first time since 1927. Their World Series opponent would be the fearsome New York Yankees, who had won eight of the last 11 Fall Classics.

Clemente finished the regular season with a .314 batting average and hit 16 home runs, just 10 fewer than he had his first fives season combined. He also made the National League All-Star team for the first time in his career, the first of his 12 selections. Now he had a chance to show just how good he really was on the grandest stage of all, the World Series.

WINNING IT ALL

Hardly anyone gave the Pirates a chance against the powerful Yankees in the World Series. (At that time, there was no playoff system in the postseason. The pennant winners in each league simply played each other in the World Series.) In 12 years under manager Casey Stengel, the Bronx Bombers had won 10 American League pennants and eight World Series titles. They won 15 straight games to end the 1960 regular season and were heavily favored against Pittsburgh.

In front of 36,676 fans at Forbes Field, the Pirates surprised everyone with a 6-4 victory in Game 1. Clemente had a single in four at bats and drove in one run.

Yet the Yankees squashed the Pirates' momentum in Game 2. Led by two homers and five RBI from Mickey Mantle, the Yankees crushed the Pirates 16-3 to tie the series at 1-1.

Back home at Yankee Stadium for Game 3, the Yankees got another homer from Mantle and a grand slam from Bobby Richardson, who knocked in six runs that day, on their way to an easy 10-0 victory. The powerhouse Yankees had outscored the Bucs 30-9 in the first three games.

The Pirates, however, showed their resiliency in Game 4, bouncing back from the two lopsided losses to earn a 3-2 win behind excellent pitching from Vernon Law.

With the series tied at 2-2, the pivotal Game 5 was played at Yankee Stadium. In front of a crowd of over 62,000, strong pitching once again carried the Pirates as starter Harvey Haddix and relief specialist Roy Face kept the Yankees' hitters down in a 5-2 win. Clemente had another single and one RBI.

The Pirates went back to Pittsburgh needing to win only one more game to capture the World Series. The Yankees would not go down easy, though.

In Game 6, future Hall of Famer Whitey Ford pitched his second shutout of the series as New York romped to a 12-0 win. Clemente had two more singles in the Yankee blowout.

Despite being outscored 46-17 and losing by margins of 16-3, 10-0, and 12-0, the Pirates managed to split the first six games of the series and to set up a decisive seventh game at Forbes Field.

In Game 7, the Pirates quickly scored four runs in the first two innings to give Law a 4-0 cushion. Yet the Yankees rallied against Law and Face in the fifth and sixth innings to take a 7-4 lead. When Clemente came to the plate in the bottom of the eighth, the Yankees were four outs away from winning the championship. They held a 7-5 lead, but the Pirates had runners on second and third base. Clemente had gotten a hit

The Pirates ended a 25-year drought by finally winning the World Series in 1960. In the seven-game Fall Classic, Clemente batted .310 with nine hits and three RBI. Here, in the first game of the series, Roberto is shown sliding into second base as New York Yankees shortstop Tony Kubek looks to apply the tag. The Pirates won the opener, 6–4.

in each of the first six games of the series, but was hitless in Game 7 until now. Clemente hit a high chopper to first baseman Bill Skowron and beat pitcher Jim Coates to the bag for an infield single that brought in another run, cutting the deficit to 7-6. Thanks to Clemente's speed and hustle, the Pirates had a chance. Hal Smith followed with a three-run homer to give the Pirates a 9-7 lead.

The Yankees refused to give up, however, scoring two runs in the top of the ninth inning to tie the game at 7-7. That set the stage for one of baseball's most historic moments. Ralph

Terry, who had gotten the final out in the Pirates' eighth inning, returned to the mound in the bottom of the ninth to finish the job and send the game into extra innings. The first man he faced was second baseman Bill Mazeroski, known more for his slick fielding skills than his accomplishments with a bat. With a count of one ball and no strikes, the Pirates' second baseman launched a long drive over the ivy-covered wall in left field to give Pittsburgh its first championship since 1935.

While the people of Pittsburgh celebrated by singing and dancing through the streets, honking their car horns, and tossing confetti from windows, the Pirates players celebrated in their clubhouse by pouring champagne on one other and hugging their teammates. Roberto Clemente dressed quickly, congratulated his teammates on the victory, and headed out of the stadium onto the streets of Pittsburgh. He spent a few hours walking around the city and celebrating with the fans.

"The biggest thrill was when I come out of the clubhouse after the last Series game and saw all those thousands of fans in the street. It was something you cannot describe. I did not feel like a player at the time. I [felt] like one of those persons, and I walked the streets among them," Clemente said in Walker's *Pride of Puerto Rico*.

SPEAKING OUT

Clemente went home a champion after the 1960 season, but he did not feel too appreciated despite an outstanding year with the Pirates. When the results of the voting for the National League Most Valuable Player award were announced, Clemente was shocked and angered to see he finished in eighth place. Teammate Dick Groat won the prestigious award, and even Pirates third baseman Don Hoak and pitcher Vernon Law also finished ahead of Clemente in the ballot.

Groat, a sure-handed fielding shortstop and a terrific team leader, led the league with a .325 batting average. Yet he had just two home runs and 50 RBI, 44 fewer than Clemente.

The Most Valuable Player winner is chosen by votes conducted by a panel of some members of the Baseball Writers Association. Clemente was furious he did not receive a single first-place vote. Clemente was bothered by the claims that he was a hypochondriac because he thought white players like the often-injured Mickey Mantle were treated more fairly, and he believed that Mantle's injuries were not scrutinized as closely as his. Clemente blamed the lack of respect in the voting on prejudice because he was a dark-skinned Puerto Rican.

"Latin American Negro ballplayers are treated today much like all Negroes were treated in baseball in the early days of the broken color barrier," Clemente told *Sport* magazine. "They are subjected to prejudices and stamped with generalizations." Clemente did not stop there. He was also not happy that he did not get offers to do commercial endorsements like white players.

"I would make a lot more money in baseball if I were a white American," he later said.

The foolishness of the MVP voters motivated Clemente to do even better. He vowed to win the batting title in 1961.

Getting Respect

George Sisler knew quite a bit about hitting. He twice led the American League in batting during the 1920s with averages of .407 and .420, finishing his career, spent mostly with the St. Louis Browns of the American League, with a lifetime average of a stunning .340. Sisler wanted Clemente to become a more patient hitter. So, as the Pirates batting coach, he spent a lot of time with Clemente during spring training in 1961. Sisler wanted to see Clemente lay off pitches outside the strike zone. Clemente had averaged only 23 walks per season over his first six years because he swung at anything close to the plate, even pitches well outside the strike zone. He was an overly aggressive hitter who found a way to hit all types of pitches, but a sharper eye could make him even more successful. Under Sisler's close supervision, Clemente made a few adjustments. He switched to a heavier bat. In theory, this was supposed to help him slow down his swing and allow him to make more contact with the ball.

Clemente was eager to start the regular season to see if the slight tweaks he made would help him become an even better hitter. The cry of "Arriba! Arriba!" became a very popular chant each time Clemente came to bat at Forbes Field in 1961. *Arriba* is a Spanish word that means "Let's go!"

Clemente did not let down the fans. He hit so well early in the season that he was selected as the starting right fielder for the National League All-Star team. Clemente played in the All-Star Game as a backup player the year before, but now he was voted a starter. It was quite an honor because players, not writers, chose the All-Stars. (Currently, baseball fans select the starting players on the All-Star teams.) Upon hearing the news, Clemente went on a hitting tear. He had five hits and drove in five runs in a game against the Chicago Cubs and had four more hits against Milwaukee two days later. Clemente went to the All-Star Game leading the league with a batting average of .357. (From 1959 to 1961, two All-Star Games were played each year.)

In the first 1961 All-Star Game, played at Candlestick Park in San Francisco, Clemente ripped a triple off Yankee ace Whitey Ford in his first at bat. Then the hard-hitting Buc got a chance to be the hero after the American League tied the score to send the game into extra innings. Facing knuckleball pitcher Hoyt Wilhelm in the bottom of the tenth inning with the scored tied and runners at first and second base, Clemente smashed a line drive to right field to score Willie Mays from second base and give the National League a 5-4 victory. After the game, reporters shunned Clemente once again. They surrounded the ever-popular Mays, who deferred the attention to Clemente. "I didn't do it. This man next to me did it. Talk to him," Mays said, as told in Walker's *Pride of Puerto Rico*. The lack of attention from the writers bothered Clemente, but he focused on being happy. He

Born in Ponce, Puerto Rico, Clemente's friend, Orlando Cepeda *(sliding)*, had a 17-year major league career, playing for the San Francisco Giants, St. Louis Cardinals, Atlanta Braves, Oakland Athletics, Boston Red Sox, and Kansas City Royals. Lifetime, Cepeda batted .297 with 379 home runs and 1,365 RBI. He was elected to the Hall of Fame in Cooperstown, New York, in 1999.

considered it a big compliment that Murtaugh, who managed the game for the National League All-Stars, let him play the entire game.

Clemente continued his strong hitting for the remainder of the season, finishing with a .351 average, fulfilling his goal of winning the batting championship. He also had 23 homers, 89 RBI, and threw out 27 runners on the base paths. Clemente also earned the Silver Bat Award for winning the hitting title and received his first Gold Glove Award, given to the best fielder at each position. Clemente would win a Gold Glove 11 more times in his career. The Pirates did not repeat as league champs, however, slumping to sixth place in the National League, after winning the pennant the previous year.

Clemente flew home for the winter on a plane with San Francisco Giant Orlando Cepeda, a native Puerto Rican who led the National League in home runs and RBI. A huge crowd of nearly 18,000 people greeted Clemente and Cepeda upon their arrival at the San Juan airport. The players were driven to Sixto Escobar Stadium and honored for their achievements. Hearing the cheers from the people made Clemente feel extremely proud. He was most thrilled to have an opportunity to celebrate his accomplishments at home in Puerto Rico.

MODEL OF CONSISTENCY

The 1962 season looked like it would be special right from the start. Clemente hit a grand slam off Jim Owens in the third inning of the season opener as the Pirates beat the Philadelphia Phillies, 6-0. Then Clemente's game-tying three-run homer against the Chicago Cubs helped the Pirates improve to 5-0. He followed up those heroics with three hits in a victory over the New York Mets, giving Pittsburgh 10 straight wins to start the season. Over the long season, the Pirates eventually cooled off, finishing fourth in the National League with 93 wins. Clemente had another excellent season, batting .312 with 10 homers and 74 RBI.

When he returned to Puerto Rico, Clemente decided to skip the winter league for the first time since he was in the Marine Reserves. The time off did not affect his performance with the Pirates in 1963 as he hit .320 with 17 homers and

76 RBI, although the Pirates slipped in the standings again, falling to eighth place in the National League with a 74-88 record. (In 1962, the National League was expanded from eight teams to 10 teams with the addition of the New York Mets and the Houston Colt .45s, now named the Houston Astros.)

This year, Clemente went back to Puerto Rico and played a full season in the winter league. He helped the San Juan Senadores win the league playoffs and he played in the International Series in Managua, Nicaragua. Clemente quickly became a fan favorite among the Nicaraguans and developed a fondness for the country.

Although the mediocre Pirates finished the 1964 season in seventh place, Clemente continued to excel. He won his second batting title with a .339 average, and his 211 hits and 40 doubles were the most he would ever have in each category. Yet Clemente was frustrated because his team had struggled almost every year since winning the World Series in 1960. "Winning is fun," he told a reporter.

THE BIG DAY

One day, while driving down a street in Puerto Rico, Roberto spied a beautiful young woman walking to the drugstore. She paid no attention to him, but he drove quickly to the drugstore and was sitting inside when she walked in. He tried to speak to her but found her to be reserved and shy. This was unusual, since he was a big star and a local hero, and he had no trouble getting girls to speak to him.

With the help of his niece, he was able to arrange a date with the young woman, Vera Christina Zabala. Seeing her was difficult because her family, especially her father, was very strict and conservative. One day, Roberto finally visited her father himself and asked permission to court Vera. Reluctantly, her father agreed. Roberto wanted this young, intelligent woman to be his wife, and before long he proposed to Vera.

A large crowd filled the church of San Fernando in Carolina, Puerto Rico, on November 14, 1964, for Roberto

Newlyweds Roberto and Vera Zabala Clemente are all smiles following their marriage on November 14, 1964. More than 1,500 people attended the services, and thousands more were on hand to celebrate the event in honor of Clemente, a national hero in his homeland.

Clemente's wedding day. Less than a year after he met Vera Zabala inside a drugstore on the other side of the plaza where the church stood, Clemente married the shy, beautiful woman he pursued so aggressively. The bride and groom were treated like royalty in Puerto Rico. Clemente was a great hero for his people. The couple moved into a house on three acres of land outside of Carolina. Yet Roberto did not get to spend all his time with his new wife.

A few weeks after getting married, Clemente took over as the manager of the San Juan Senadores. He also played for the team but less often than in the past. Clemente also was busy setting up baseball clinics for young children in Puerto Rico, and he often visited sick kids at local hospitals.

At home, Clemente enjoyed doing repairs just to keep his hands busy. On one occasion, however, he probably should have hired someone to do the work for him. While mowing his lawn one afternoon, Clemente was injured when a rock shot up and hit him in the thigh. He stopped playing winter ball, hoping the time off would allow his leg to heal. When it came time for the Puerto Rican All-Star Game, Clemente felt obligated to make an appearance for the fans. "Without Roberto Clemente, how could it be an All-Star Game?" was the common reaction from people who wanted Roberto to play. Clemente got a loud ovation when he came to bat as a pinch hitter. He could hardly walk, but he lined a single to right field and limped to first base. Before he got there, Clemente's leg collapsed under him, and he fell to the ground in pain. He was rushed to the hospital and doctors had to operate to drain a pool of blood in his thigh.

The surgery left Clemente weakened. Shortly before spring training opened, Clemente developed a high fever and again had to be hospitalized. At first, the Pirates were angry that Clemente had not reported to camp on time and threatened to fine him $100 per each day he missed. They finally relented after learning the nature of his illness. Clemente's doctor advised him to sit out the 1965 season, and his wife thought he should take a one-year retirement to regain his health. A stubborn Clemente would not listen, however. "I like baseball," he said, according to Walker's *Pride of Puerto Rico*. "I love baseball and I know I have to play. It is my life."

TOUGHING IT OUT

The Pirates had a new manager for the 1965 season. Harry Walker replaced Danny Murtaugh, who stepped down for health reasons. Walker had a different philosophy than Murtaugh. He was friendlier with players, so Clemente was happy with the change in approach. Walker also was a hitting expert. He led the National League with a .361 batting average in 1947 and enjoyed lecturing on hitting. Clemente was an attentive listener.

Clemente's injury and illness during the winter clearly affected his performance early in the season. He had no homers by the middle of May and his batting average was down to .257.

Unfortunately, the relationship between Walker and Clemente soured when the manager gave his star player a rest during a series in St. Louis. After a Cardinals announcer told Clemente that Walker said he had no reason to be sitting on the bench, Clemente demanded a trade for the first time in his career. Fortunately for the Pirates organization and the fans, Walker smoothed over his relationship with Clemente very quickly. Suddenly, the Pirates started winning again, and Clemente was hitting as well as ever. He had a hit in 33 of 34 games at one point, raising his average to .340. Meanwhile, the Pirates went 20-2 to climb out of last place.

They finished the season in third place, and Clemente somehow overcame his health problems to win his second consecutive batting title with a .329 average. He also became the fifth player to win three batting championships, joining Honus Wagner, Rogers Hornsby, Paul Waner, and Stan Musial.

A True
Leader

Roberto Clemente looked around at his magnificent new house in Rio Piedras, a suburb outside San Juan, and knew he had everything any man could want: a beautiful and loyal wife, a healthy son, a spectacular home, and a lucrative career playing a sport he dreamed about as a kid. He was beloved in Puerto Rico, and the people in Pittsburgh adored him too.

Yet Clemente still had not gained the same respect among fans in the United States. He had won three National League batting titles, batted over .300 for six consecutive seasons, earned five straight Gold Glove Awards, played in the All-Star Game six years in a row, and helped the Pirates win a world championship. Still, the "Puerto Rican hot dog" label stuck with him. Some critics said he was not a clutch hitter. Others argued he was not a power hitter because he did not

Light-hitting Matty Alou had only minimal success in the majors—until he joined the Pirates in 1966, when Clemente took Alou under his wing and began mentoring the 28-year-old. From that year on, Alou became one of baseball's top hitters, winning the National League batting title in 1966 with a .342 average and hitting over .300 seven times. Matty's brothers, Felipe and Jesus, and his nephew, Moises, also played in the major leagues.

hit many home runs. Many still questioned his desire to play through pain.

Clemente would get very angry when anyone did not believe he was sick or injured. They would see him smash line drives all over the field and wonder how his elbow or back or anything else could possibly be hurt. As for the lack of home runs, a big part of the problem was cavernous Forbes Field. Even Hank Aaron or Babe Ruth would have trouble hitting balls out of a stadium so big.

Before the 1966 season, Clemente had an important conversation with manager Harry Walker during spring training. Walker told Clemente he had to hit for more power for the team to be successful that year. He also asked Clemente to be a leader for the younger players. "You need to set an example for the other players. If they see you hustle, they hustle, too," as told in Walker's *Pride of Puerto Rico*. Clemente replied: "I always hustle." Walker explained that he meant showing leadership in other ways, such as tutoring younger players. The message was clear. Clemente was ready to show he could be a mentor.

Clemente's first project was a young hitter named Matty Alou. The Pirates had acquired Alou in a trade with the San Francisco Giants. A small player with a short, compact left-handed swing, Alou unsuccessfully tried to hit home runs in San Francisco. In six seasons, he had just 14 homers. Clemente worked with Alou day after day in spring training, trying to turn him into a line-drive hitter who sprayed the ball around to all fields. Alou, who was from the Dominican Republic, quickly applied Clemente's instruction.

POWER AND PATIENCE

While Alou took over the role of being the singles hitter on the Pirates, Clemente was determined to prove he could hit for more power. Only once in his first 11 years did he have more than 17 homers, hitting 23 in 1961. To be a successful power hitter meant that Clemente had to be more patient at the plate.

He had to be willing to draw a walk if a pitcher did not give him anything good to hit. New York Yankees slugger Mickey Mantle walked more than 100 times in a season eight out of nine years between 1954 and 1962. Meanwhile, Clemente never walked more than 51 times in his first 11 seasons.

In a late April game, the Pirates trailed the Chicago Cubs 4-3 with two outs in the top of the ninth inning when Clemente came to the plate against relief pitcher Ted Abernathy. The first two pitches were strikes, and Clemente fell behind in the count 0-2. Then he managed to take three straight pitches outside the strike zone to run a full count and fouled off eight in a row to stay alive. Finally, Clemente drew a walk to keep the game going. Willie Stargell followed with a double to score Clemente, and the Pirates went on to win the game in extra innings. It was Clemente's walk that started the rally, a sign that he could help the Pirates win a game by showing discipline at the plate instead of getting a hit every time up.

Nearing the end of May, Clemente was slumping. He had only 3 hits in 16 at bats and was batting .295 with only three homers when Harry Walker decided to give him a rest. Clemente did not start four straight games before returning to play the second game of a doubleheader against the Houston Astros on May 28. Two days later, Clemente hit a solo homer off Chicago's Dick Ellsworth to help the Pirates beat the Cubs 3-2. It was the first time he had gone deep since connecting off Sandy Koufax in a loss to Los Angeles 16 days earlier.

Now Clemente was starting to get hot. During an 11-game home stand in early June, he batted .444, raising his average to .330. He also hit six home runs, including two long drives to right-center field in Forbes Field that measured more than 436 feet (133 meters) from the plate.

Led by Clemente, the Pirates pushed the Dodgers and Giants for first place. The three teams remained locked in a tight battle throughout the summer. Pittsburgh had a slight edge over the Giants and Dodgers when the Cubs came to town on September 2. Leading 1-0 in the fifth inning, Clemente stepped to the plate to face Ferguson Jenkins. With one out and two runners on base, he smashed a line drive into the seats in right-center field for a three-run homer that tied his career high at 23. It also gave him 101 RBI, the first time he had surpassed 100 RBI in a season. Lastly, and more important, it was the 2,000th career hit for Clemente, making him the ninth major league player to reach that total. Clemente was proud of this accomplishment, but he wanted to celebrate another championship more than anything.

The Pirates faded down the stretch and finished in third place behind the Giants and Dodgers, who won the National League pennant. Clemente finished his best all-around season with a .317 batting average, 29 homers, and 119 RBIs. His protégé, Matty Alou, won the batting title with a .342 average.

MOST VALUABLE PLAYER

After being snubbed in the voting for Most Valuable Player in 1960, Clemente figured the baseball writers would never give him the respect he deserved. He was quite surprised and overjoyed to learn the sportswriters voted him National League MVP after the 1966 season. Clemente beat out Sandy Koufax, who won 27 games and pitched 27 complete games for the first-place Dodgers. Many considered the award was long overdue for Clemente. He considered it a validation for all Puerto Ricans.

"Always, they said Babe Ruth was the best there was. They said you'd really have to be something to be like Babe Ruth. But Babe Ruth was an American player. What we needed was a Puerto Rican player they could say that about, someone to look up to and try to equal," Clemente said after winning the award. "This makes me happy because now the people feel that if I could do it, then they could do it. The kids have someone to look to and to follow. That's why I like to work with kids so much. I show them what baseball has done for me and maybe they will work harder and try harder and be better men."

The year 1966 was a highlight in Roberto Clemente's remarkable career, batting .317 with 202 hits, a career-high 29 home runs, and 119 RBI. For his outstanding performance, Clemente won the National League Most Valuable Player Award. Here, Clemente raps out another hit, this one against the New York Mets in a game played in August of that year.

Winning the MVP Award earned Clemente a nice raise in his salary. He signed a new contract with the Pirates that made him one of only five players making $100,000 per year. The others were Willie Mays, Hank Aaron, Mickey Mantle, and Frank Robinson. Of course, Clemente wanted to show everyone he was worth every single penny.

EARNING BIG BUCKS

Winning the MVP Award only made Clemente hungry to play even better the following season. Certainly he was not someone to sit on his accomplishments. Still, the Pirates started slowly in 1967, losing five of their first eight games. Then Clemente's hitting helped them win five straight games, and he was batting .358 after getting three hits, including a homer, against the St. Louis Cardinals on May 1.

Pittsburgh was very inconsistent over the next two months, resulting in the firing of manager Harry Walker in July. Danny Murtaugh was renamed manager, returning to his old job. Clemente once had problems with Walker when the manager gave him a few days off and supposedly criticized him for not playing hurt. But the two smoothed over their relationship and got along well after that. In fact, Clemente really liked playing for Walker. "I got along with Harry so [well] because he thinks baseball the way I think and I'm glad," Clemente said in Markusen's *Roberto Clemente: The Great One.*

Before Walker was fired, Clemente gave his manager a strong endorsement. "I am playing hard because of him," he said. "He treats me like a human being. He makes me feel wanted, makes me feel important. He gives me peace of mind." Walker helped Clemente become a more aggressive fielder, encouraging him to charge ground balls harder. He also helped him develop into more of a power hitter by convincing him not to cut down on his swing and be content with hitting singles.

With Murtaugh now at the helm, people wondered whether the switch would affect the team. Clemente and Murtaugh had their issues in the past, but both men were now a bit older, wiser, and more mature. Clemente had no choice but to accept the move. "I can play for any manager," he said. Unfortunately, the managerial change did not help the Pirates. Even though Clemente batted .357 to win his fourth batting title, Pittsburgh finished in sixth place in the National League.

Clemente also had 23 homers and 110 RBI to go with the highest batting average of his career. He headed back to Puerto Rico and decided to play winter ball after taking the previous year off.

NO HIRED HELP

Back home in Rio Piedras, Clemente was doing work on a two-leveled patio at his house. As he was climbing to the second level, one of the iron bars broke away from the wall. Clemente crashed to the ground below. He landed on the back of his neck and rolled over on his throwing shoulder, continuing to roll until a low wall overlooking a steep cliff stopped him. Clemente could have been paralyzed or even killed in that fall. "I'm lucky to be alive," he said afterward.

GETTING PAID

Roberto Clemente never forgot how hard his father worked on a sugarcane plantation to provide for his family. For Clemente, playing baseball allowed him to easily support the ones he loved.

In January 1967, Clemente went to Pittsburgh for a series of winter banquets to promote the upcoming season. While there, Clemente sat down with Pirates general manager, Joe Brown, to negotiate his contract. He had just won the National League's Most Valuable Player Award after hitting .317 with career highs in homers (29) and runs batted in (119). Certainly a nice raise was in order.

During a two-hour meeting at an upscale hotel, a milestone deal was reached that would pay Clemente $100,000 a year, making him the highest-paid player in team history.

It was a staggering amount of money at that time, much more than the 45 cents per day Don Melchor earned for laboring on the plantations. Only four other players in baseball made that much money. They were Willie Mays, Hank Aaron, Frank Robinson, and Mickey Mantle.

Clemente tore a muscle in his right shoulder in the fall, making it very difficult and extremely painful to swing a bat. As a result, he had a tough time early in the 1968 season. By the end of May, he was batting only .222 with five homers. His average rose slightly to .245 by the All-Star break. For the first time in nine years, Clemente was not chosen to represent the National League at the Midsummer Classic.

A proud man who refused to give up, Clemente rebounded with a strong second half and finished the season with a .291 average, 18 homers, and 57 RBI. These were respectable numbers for most players, but it was the first time since 1959 that Clemente had not batted above .300. The Pirates finished in sixth place again. This time, Larry Shepard was the manager because Murtaugh had retired.

Clemente was a very generous man no matter how much he earned. He donated money to the poor, generously tipped employees and offered financial assistance to his niece and nephew. Sometimes he even helped teammates.

"Baseball has enabled me to support 11 people and it has given me an education," Clemente said. "It has brought me a measure of fame and money. I'm very grateful."[*]

Brown did not have any trouble dealing with Clemente over his contract. In fact, the two men briefly discussed finances during their meeting. They talked about other topics and spent only a few minutes on Clemente's salary. "Never had any problems with him. Never came close to a holdout,"[**] Brown said.

Of course, Clemente wanted to prove to the fans and everyone else that he was worth the big salary. He batted .357 in 1967, the highest average of his career.

[*] Quoted in Bruce Markusen, *Roberto Clemente: The Great One* (Champaign, IL: Sagamore Publishing, 1998), 160.

[**] Ibid.

After the season, Clemente seriously contemplated retirement again. He was 34 years old now, and he had two sons with a third child on the way. Having a subpar season made him feel that he was cheating the fans because he had not given them his best. Yet Vera Clemente convinced her husband not to make such an important decision out of frustration. She told him to give it one more year. Roberto listened to his wife's advice and took a season off from winter ball to allow his body time to heal and recover fully.

MEETING THE COMMISSIONER

In 1969, Bowie Kuhn was named Major League Baseball's fifth commissioner. Kuhn had previously served as a lawyer to major league owners for 20 years. That spring, Kuhn traveled to several spring training sites to visit different teams. His first encounter with Clemente left a lasting impression on the rookie commissioner. "He was a very commanding man, commanding in manner of style and appearance; even in the way he moved, he was commanding," Kuhn said, according to Bruce Markusen's *Roberto Clemente: The Great One.* "And I was struck immediately with the fact that he had none of the sort of reticence that ballplayers are apt to have when talking to the commissioner—not at all. He spoke to the commissioner and everybody else as equals, that's the way he was. And I don't say that in any sense critically. It was refreshing and it was all done with excellent style."

Kuhn did not have a long conversation with Clemente. No one except possibly his wife, Vera, talked to Clemente at length. His style was to keep it short and simple. Yet everything Clemente said had substance. Kuhn spoke to Clemente often throughout his reign as commissioner. Each time it was the same. "Most conversations with him were not memorable in terms of what he said, but in terms of Clemente being Clemente," Kuhn said. "Not in terms of the content. Simply in terms of Clemente—you were having a conversation with the king."

The Great One

Taking the winter off helped Roberto Clemente heal physically. He knew his right shoulder was just fine when he hit a long home run in a spring training intrasquad game early in the spring. (An intrasquad game is a game played between two teams, each team comprised of players from the main team; in this case, the Pittsburgh Pirates.) Soon, however, Clemente injured his left shoulder while diving for a ball in a game against the Boston Red Sox.

The point of playing exhibition games is to get players in shape for the regular season and for management to determine who will make the final roster when the season starts. A lot of competition for the limited spots on the roster is often created between the players. Starters rarely play an entire exhibition game, and it is not unusual to see some players play at less than full speed. No one wants to get hurt in a meaningless game.

Clemente, however, was too proud not to give it his all. He would always pursue a fly ball at full speed, risking his body to catch the ball, even though it did not matter who won or lost the game. The injury he suffered against the Red Sox was such an example of his all-out style.

The shoulder injury lingered as the Pirates began the regular season. Adding to his woes, Clemente soon suffered a pulled muscle in his left leg in a game in early April. This surely was not the way Clemente wanted to start the year, especially after having a subpar season the year before. On April 13, the Pirates were playing a home game against the Philadelphia Phillies. Clemente had one of the worst games of his career. He struck out in his first at bat and grounded into a double play each of his next two times up to lower his batting average to .190. He also let a ball go between his legs in right field for an error in the top of the eighth inning.

When Clemente came to the plate in the bottom of the eighth, a strange sound filled the stadium. It started slowly at first, then picked up momentum: "Booooooooo! Booooooooo! Booooooooo!" For the first time in his career, in his 15 seasons with the Pirates, Roberto Clemente heard boos from the home fans at Forbes Field. He stepped out of the batter's box, took his helmet off, and waved it to the crowd. Suddenly some of the boos turned to cheers. Clemente got back in the box and eventually drew a walk. He scored on Willie Stargell's two-run homer to tie the game. The Pirates scored another run to win 6-5.

Afterward, everyone wanted to know what Clemente meant by waving his helmet to the fans. "I wasn't trying to be smart with them," Clemente said. "I just wanted to show them that if they wanted to boo, it was all right with me. I haven't been swinging the bat and they have a right to get down on me. I don't remember it ever happening before, but I guess every ballplayer hears it sooner or later."[10]

Not only had Clemente been a favorite among fans throughout his career, he was very friendly with them. He tried his best to personally answer all the fan mail he received. He went out of his way to sign autographs every chance he got, especially if the seekers were children.

If any player deserved a break during bad times, it was Clemente. To his credit, he did not let the jeers bother him. He knew it would not last long, either.

BRUSH WITH DEATH

Clemente's struggles at the plate continued into late May. He was batting just .242 when the Pirates headed out to the West Coast for 10 games against the Dodgers, the San Diego Padres, and the Giants.

After losing three straight to Los Angeles, the Pirates went to San Diego. It was there that Clemente was involved in one of the most bizarre, and scary, incidents of his life. Following a phone conversation with his wife in which he again expressed his desire to retire and Vera again persuading him to stick it out a little longer, Clemente left his hotel room and went down to the lobby. He ran into Stargell, who was eating chicken. Stargell told Clemente he bought the food at a place down the road. Clemente went out to buy some for himself. On his way back to the hotel, a car pulled up to Clemente and one of the four men inside pointed a gun at him and ordered him to get inside.

The bandits drove Clemente to a deserted spot in the mountains. They took $250 in cash from his wallet, made him strip off his clothes, and took the All-Star ring he had from the 1961 game. Clemente thought he was going to be killed. His entire life flashed before his eyes. He thought of his wife and children in Puerto Rico and his baseball career. He would not see them again. He would never play again. Then he heard one of the robbers speaking Spanish. Clemente pleaded with them in his native language and told them he was a major league baseball player. After they checked his wallet and discovered who he was, they gave back his clothes and his money and ring. They even drove him back to the hotel. Thankful to be alive, Clemente started to walk back to the hotel from the spot he was dropped off only to hear the car zoom back toward him. He thought the robbers had changed their minds. Instead, one of the men called out to him and gave him the chicken he had bought.

Bill Christine, a writer for the *Pittsburgh Press*, broke the news of the incident 15 months later because Clemente never told anyone what happened. Many members of the media, fans, and even some of his teammates were skeptical of the incredible story. Christine checked the records of the San Diego police department and found that Clemente had indeed reported the abduction to authorities at the time.

Soon after his harrowing experience, Clemente regained his hitting stroke. By the middle of June, his average was up to .314. Still, he heard more criticism about his desire to play in spite of injuries. Finally, he lashed out at the critics. "I kill myself for this club," Clemente said. "They make sarcastic remarks on TV, say I'm not hurt, that I should play when I have injury, that I'm not a team player."

The negative remarks only fueled Clemente to do more. He finished the season batting .345, second only to Pete Rose, who batted .348 for the Cincinnati Reds. Clemente also had 19 homers and 91 RBI. The Pirates finished in third place.

BACK TO MURTAUGH

The results of the voting for the Player of the Decade were announced following the 1969 season. Roberto Clemente figured he would be a strong candidate for first place. During the 1960s, Clemente played in the All-Star Game nine times, and he won a National League MVP Award. He also won nine Gold Glove Awards and four batting titles and helped the Pirates capture the World Series championship in 1960. He always had a difficult time getting recognition, and the voting for the Player of the Decade was no different. Dodgers' pitcher Sandy Koufax finished first in the voting, followed by sluggers Mickey Mantle, Willie Mays, and Hank Aaron. Clemente finished in ninth place, another sign of disrespect in his eyes.

It had been 10 years since the Pirates made the playoffs as the team headed into the 1970 season. After splitting the previous year with two managers, Larry Shepard and Alex Grammas, general manager, Joe Brown, decided the team needed more of Danny Murtaugh.

Clemente had a tenuous relationship with Murtaugh during his first two stints as manager. Murtaugh publicly questioned Clemente's many injuries, directly challenged the superstar, and even accused him of faking an injury once when he asked out of the lineup. No wonder Clemente expressed an open dislike for the manager. Yet Murtaugh also realized how important Clemente was to the Pirates, not only for his playing skills but for his leadership. No matter the race or ethnicity of his teammates, Clemente served as a role model for other players. He unified everyone in the locker room.

Instead of alienating Clemente, Murtaugh confided in him. They did not become best of friends, but they learned to coexist for the benefit of the team. The Pirates started slowly under Murtaugh, with a seven-game losing streak in early May dropping their record to 11-14. They remained inconsistent over the next six weeks and were 31-33 after finishing a trip to the West Coast. Boarding their plane in Los Angeles, everyone on the team knew the next two weeks would be an emotional time. The Pirates were returning home to Pittsburgh to play the final 11 games at Forbes Field before moving to the new Three Rivers Stadium.

GOOD-BYE, FORBES

Roberto Clemente spent half his life playing at Forbes Field. Built under the direction of Pirates owner, Barney Dreyfuss, and named for General John Forbes, who served in the French and Indian War, Forbes Field was home to the Pittsburgh Pirates for parts of 62 seasons, from mid-1909 to mid-1970. Forbes was one of the first steel-and-concrete baseball parks in the country and was known for its large dimensions: 457 feet (139 meters) from home plate to the left-center field wall. Clemente certainly would have hit more home runs if he played in another park, but he knew how to take advantage of the spacious outfield to get doubles and triples.

The last games played at Forbes Field would be on June 28, a doubleheader against the Chicago Cubs. Clemente played in the first game but not the second one. Fittingly, he doubled and scored the winning run in the first contest. The Pirates also won the second game, closing out their history at Forbes Field with seven straight victories. They continued their winning ways on the road, going 10-4 and solidifying their position in first place in the National League East.

When they returned home after the All-Star break in mid-July, the Pirates moved into Three Rivers Stadium. An ultramodern stadium built at the junction of the Ohio, Allegheny, and Monongahela rivers, it had an evenly shaped playing field and an artificial turf instead of a natural grass field. The dimensions were much smaller than Forbes Field, with straightaway center field only 400 feet (122 meters) from home plate.

Clemente quickly adapted to the quick surface of artificial turf, learning how to play the hops to cut balls off in the gap. A week after Three Rivers Stadium opened, the Pirates held a day to honor Clemente before a game against the Houston Astros. It was Roberto Clemente Night, and 43,290 fans, many of whom were Puerto Rican, came out to celebrate their hero.

Roberto's parents, wife, and three children were among those in the crowd. It was an emotional night for everyone. Clemente had two hits, made two outstanding catches in right field, and the Pirates beat the Astros 11-0 to cap a perfect evening.

Roberto's entire family was on hand to celebrate Roberto Clemente Night at Three Rivers Stadium, in Pittsburgh, on July 24, 1970. Featured in this photo are *(left to right):* his parents, Melchor and Luisa; Clemente holding Roberto Jr.; Luis and Enrique; and Vera.

PLAYING HURT

A number of injuries forced Clemente out of the lineup several times during the stretch run. He tried to play through the pain as often as possible. "I wanted to rest him, but he insisted on playing," Murtaugh said, according to Paul Walker's *Pride of Puerto Rico.*

Clemente had five hits in consecutive games in August to become the first player to have 10 hits in two games. Yet he finally could not continue to play injured, and he missed all but seven games in September. The Pirates managed to stay in first place, winning the National League East Division title. Clemente finished the season with a .352 average, 14 homers, and 60 RBI in only 108 games. Now it was time to face the Cincinnati Reds in the playoffs.

It was a best-of-five series. The first team to win three games would represent the National League in the World Series against the American League opponent. The Pirates, however, were held in check by outstanding Cincinnati pitching, mustering only three runs in the series, and they were swept in three games. Clemente had just three hits in 14 at bats. The bitter taste of losing the series lingered for a while. It also made Clemente yearn even more to play in one more World Series before he retired.

After the season, a reporter asked Clemente if he was contemplating retirement. He was now 36 years old, and most players his age already were out of the game. "Let's see," he said, "I hit three hundred forty-five last year and three hundred fifty-two this year. No, I don't think I want to quit now."[11]

Clemente, however, nearly changed his mind. His father, Don Melchor, fell seriously ill that winter. Yet before his operation, Don Melchor inspired his son by telling Roberto that the Pirates needed the star right fielder to make the World Series again, especially after coming so close in 1970.

AGE IS ONLY A NUMBER

At 36, Clemente was still one of the best hitters in the game. Sure, he was older and tired and more susceptible to injuries, yet he could still hit line drives all over the field. The younger Pirates had a lot of fun with Clemente in 1971, especially since the team started winning early and was cruising toward another first-place finish. One day, catcher Manny Sanguillen and star pitcher Dock Ellis were clowning around while Clemente was getting a massage before a game. Sanguillen slid across the floor, imitating Clemente. "Did you see Clemente slide last night?"Sanguillen said. "I want to go help him up, the old man!"[12] Clemente pretended not to hear them, but he was laughing along inside as well. There was excellent team chemistry on the Pirates. Players liked each other and got along well, and they were winning quite a bit of games.

Sanguillen batted .319, Stargell led the league with 48 homers, and Clemente had another outstanding season. He batted .341 with 13 homers and 86 RBI. The Pirates won 97 games to capture the National League East title for the second straight season, setting up a meeting with the San Francisco Giants for the pennant.

The first game was played at Candlestick Park in San Francisco. Behind Gaylord Perry's pitching, the Giants won 5-4 to take a lead in the series. Clemente was not discouraged. "We'll win this and the World Series," he said. "You just wait and see."[13]

The Pirates made Clemente look like a prophet. They swept the next three games to advance to the World Series. Clemente had three RBI in the final game against the Giants, including a hard single up the middle that drove in the go-ahead run.

CLEMENTE'S SHOWCASE

Just as they were in 1960 against the New York Yankees, the Pirates were heavy underdogs against the Baltimore Orioles in the 1971 World Series. The Orioles had an impressive arsenal of pitching, featuring four starters who won at least 20 games each. A powerful offense was led by Boog Powell, Frank and Brooks Robinson, Merv Rettenmund, and Dave Johnson. Baltimore finished the regular season with 11 straight wins and swept the Oakland A's in three games in the American League Championship Series. Somehow, the Pirates needed to find a way to stop the Orioles' momentum to have a chance to be champions again. The night before Game 1, Clemente and Stargell were riding an elevator together. Clemente turned calmly to Stargell and said, "I will carry the team."[14]

Clemente's confidence did not help the Pirates much as the Orioles won the first two games of the series at Baltimore's Memorial Stadium. Since 1903, only five teams had come back to win the World Series after losing the first two games. Frustrated by their lack of hitting and the Orioles' dominance, the Pirates looked like a beaten team. Clemente would not let them accept defeat, however. "Don't worry," he told them. "I'll

ROBERTO CLEMENTE NIGHT

Roberto Clemente looked up at the crowd of 44,000 people and felt right at home in the Pirates' new stadium. Fans in the right field stands wore big white straw hats just like the *pavas* worn by Puerto Rican workers in the sugar fields. On the field were Roberto's wife, Vera, and their three children, Roberto Jr., Luis, and Enrique. Roberto's parents, Don Melchor and Dona Luisa, sat beside them. Heriberto Nieves, the mayor of the Puerto Rican city Carolina, also was in attendance. It was July 24, 1970, Roberto Clemente Night at Three Rivers Stadium.

Once the ceremony began, the Latino players on the Pirates each walked up to Clemente and embraced him. A young Puerto Rican businessman named Juan Jimenez gave Clemente a scroll with 300,000 signatures from the people of Puerto Rico. Other gifts included trophies and a new car. A charitable man, Clemente asked that money be donated to the disabled children at Pittsburgh's Children's Hospital.

When it came time for Clemente to speak, his eyes became filled with tears. "I want to dedicate this triumph to all the mothers in Puerto Rico," he said. "I haven't the words to express my gratitude. I only ask that those who are watching this program be close to their parents, ask for their blessing and get you up when we get to Pittsburgh. I will hit those Baltimore pitchers like we're taking batting practice."[15]

Backed by a strong outing from pitcher Steve Blass, the Pirates won the next game 5-3. Game 4 was the first night game in World Series history. With more than 60 million fans watching on television, the Pirates tied the series with a 4-3 victory. After the game, New York sportswriter Dick Young wrote: "The best ballplayer in the World Series, maybe the whole world, is Roberto Clemente."[16] Clemente finally was getting his due respect. Now he wanted another championship ring.

embrace. . . . And those friends who are watching or listening, shake hands in the friendship that unites all Puerto Ricans."*

Clemente looked over at his parents. Don Melchor was 90 years old, thin, and frail. This trip to Pittsburgh was his first time on an airplane. He would not miss witnessing a special night honoring his son. Clemente would not disappoint his dad or the thousands of fans who came to the game, rapping out two hits, making one sliding catch and another diving catch, as the Pirates romped to an 11-0 victory over the Astros.

After the game, Clemente explained his tears during the ceremony. "I am not ashamed to cry," he said. "I would say a man never cries from pain or disappointment. But if you know the history of our island, you ought to remember we're a sentimental people. I don't have the words to say how I feel when I step on that field and know that so many people are behind me, and know that so many represent my island and Latin America."**

* Quoted in Paul Robert Walker, *Pride of Puerto Rico: The Life of Roberto Clemente* (New York: Odyssey Classics, 1991), 124–125.

** Ibid., 126.

Nelson Briles delivered a spectacular pitching performance, a three-hit shutout, to lead the Pirates to a 4-0 victory in Game 5, putting the underdogs within one victory of winning it all.

Yet the Orioles would not bow down easily. They won the next game 3-2, despite a triple and home run by Clemente, to force a seventh game.

It was a cool, overcast Sunday afternoon for Game 7 at Memorial Field. Steve Blass was on the mound for the Pirates against Mike Cuellar. Both pitchers were on their game in the early innings, neither allowing a hit. When Clemente came to the plate in the top of the fourth, Cuellar had retired the first 11 hitters. Clemente ended that streak by driving a home run over the left-field fence to give the Pirates a 1-0 lead. Another Pirate run in the eighth inning made it 2-0, but the Orioles cut it to 2-1 in the bottom of the eighth. No problem, however. Blass set them down on eight pitches in the ninth, and the Pirates were world champions again.

Before the game, Clemente had confided in a scout that he planned to retire if the Pirates won. As he ran off the field, Clemente spotted his wife in the stands. One more time, she convinced him to keep playing. "Don't quit now. Baseball's your life,"[17] she said.

Clemente was named MVP of the series. He batted .414 with two homers, one triple, and two doubles. "I want everyone to know this is how I play all the time," Clemente said afterward. "All season, every season, I gave everything I have to this game. The press call me a crybaby, a hypochondriac. They say that I'm not a team player. Now everyone knows the way Roberto Clemente plays. They saw me in the World Series. Mentally, I will be a different person now."

ONE LAST SEASON

Seemingly, the older Clemente got, the more he hit. Clemente batted .345, .352, and .341 after turning 34. He entered the

September 30, 1972, marked another landmark in Clemente's career when he picked up career hit number 3,000, against Jon Matlack of the New York Mets in a game won by the Pirates, 5–0. Roberto's fourth-inning double, shown here, was to be the last regular season hit by the Pittsburgh superstar.

1972 season needing only 118 hits to reach the 3,000-hit milestone, one of baseball's most-esteemed plateaus.

Before the season, Clemente was on a plane with Sanguillen. "Sangy, I've got to get those 3,000 hits this year," he said to his friend and teammate. "I might get sick or die, and no other Latin will do it."[18] Heading into the final 26 games, Clemente was 25 hits short of the magic number. He got hot the final month. Hit number 2,999 came off Phillies left-hander Steve Carlton in Philadelphia on September 28.

Clemente asked to come out of the lineup after that hit because the Pirates were going home, and he wanted to get the milestone in front of the home fans. Facing rookie pitcher Jon Matlack of the New York Mets on September 30, 1972, a day after Tom Seaver kept him hitless, Clemente ripped a line-drive double for his 3,000th career hit in front of a late-season Three Rivers crowd of only 13,117. The fans gave him a standing ovation, and the umpire presented Clemente with the ball.

Clemente would have to wait for his next hit because he did not play the final games of the season, in order to get some rest for the playoffs, which the Pirates made with a 96-59 record. The Pirates, however, lost an exciting five-game series to the Cincinnati Reds. For Clemente, it would be the end. He never got a chance to get hit number 3,001.

The Fallen Hero

Throughout his career, Roberto Clemente became almost as well known for his charitable works and his big heart as for his deadly bat and powerful throwing arm. He once said, "If you have a chance to accomplish something that will make things better for people coming behind you, and you don't do that, then you are wasting your time on this earth."[19] It was the mantra by which he lived.

This was not a surprise to anyone who knew Clemente's family. Coincidentally, the Spanish word *clemente* means "clemency," another way of saying "merciful." Roberto's mother, Luisa Walker, was a religious woman who prayed regularly and believed in charitable works. She lived a life that incorporated kindness and benevolence. Even though the Clemente family did not have much, Roberto Clemente grew up seeing his mother giving food to the poorest children of the neighborhood whenever she could.

Whenever the Pirates played in different cities, Clemente visited various hospitals in which sick children were being treated, some of them for terminal illnesses. In fact, when he received fan mail, he often sorted out the ones from children according to the cities in which they were being hospitalized, so that he could plan a visit when he was next scheduled to be in the same town. He tried to make sure that the visits were private, that no television cameras or reporters were around, so that he could spend personal time speaking with the children, encouraging them.

For Clemente, one of his top priorities and the cause closest to his heart were the children of Puerto Rico. He had grown up as a Puerto Rican youth, in all the poverty that still plagued the island and its troubled economy, but he had been one of the lucky ones. Baseball had provided him with a path for escaping that poverty and making a better life for his own family, but he could never forget his origins. He often used public appearances as an opportunity to bring awareness of the plight of Puerto Rican youth to American audiences. For years he had spent his free time sponsoring baseball clinics for young people all over Puerto Rico, to try to hook them on sports as a positive way to spend their own free time, rather than falling into the trap of drugs and violence. After the Pirates won the World Series, for example, Clemente was honored at a dinner at Mamma Leone's restaurant in New York City. He was being recognized with an award for outstanding player of the series by *Sport Magazine*.

During his speech, Clemente talked about a dream he had envisioned to help the children of Puerto Rico. He imagined building and maintaining a sports city, built on the island, that would include stadiums and fields to help promote sports as both a career path and a productive pastime for young people.

"I don't want anything for myself," he said that evening, after accepting the award, "but through me I can help lots of people. They spend millions of dollars for dope control in Puerto Rico. But they attack the problem after the problem is there. Why don't they attack it before it starts? You try to get kids so they don't become addicts, and it would help to get them interested in sports and give them somewhere to learn to play them. I want to have three baseball fields, a swimming pool, basketball, tennis, a lake where fathers and sons can get together. . . ."[20]

The benefits of such a sports city would be tremendous, he explained, and not just for the children of Puerto Rico. "I feel the United States should have something like this all over. If I was the President of the United States I would build a sports city and take in kids of all ways of life. What we want to do is exchange kids with every city in the United States and show all the kids how to live and play with other kids. I been going out to different towns, different neighborhoods. I get kids together and talk about the importance of sports, the importance of being a good citizen, the importance of respecting their mother and father."[21]

If he could get the money he needed, Clemente claimed that evening, he would quit baseball and work full-time at making the dream of a sports city in Puerto Rico a reality.

THE QUAKE

The country of Nicaragua is located in Central America. Its western border is the Pacific Ocean, and its eastern border is the Caribbean Sea. In the middle of the night on December 23, 1972, a powerful earthquake ripped through the capital city of Managua. With the first tremor, writes biographer David Maraniss, "The earth shuddered from side to side. Soon a second rumble, more up and down than horizontal, like some gargantuan creature bursting to the surface from deep underground. Later a third quake, again up and down,

On December 23, 1972, a two-hour earthquake ripped through the Nicaraguan capital of Managua. Eighty percent of the city's buildings were destroyed, and estimates place the death toll as high as 10,000. This aerial view, taken two days later, shows the devastation of the city.

more violent than the second—and in a thunderous spasm the city collapsed on itself."[22] In fact, much of the central district of Managua was completely flattened.

The British Broadcasting Corporation (BBC) reported that the devastating earthquake, which measured 6.5 on the Richter scale, lasted two hours total, destroying 80 percent of the buildings in Managua. Two of the city's three main hospitals were also destroyed, making rescue efforts exceedingly problematic. As workers dug through the rubble in the hopes of finding survivors, it was almost impossible to get medical treatment to those victims who were actually found alive.

The main shock was followed by several powerful aftershocks and, while electricity was cut off, a second ravaging problem occurred: fire. Fires sparked by the quake spread rapidly throughout the city, making conditions even worse for survivors and rescue workers.

In total, between 5,000 and 10,000 Nicaraguans died, and more than 20,000 were injured. Of the city's 400,000 residents, more than half became homeless. A mass evacuation of the city began, although organizing the mass exodus of so many people was fraught with its own set of complications. How can such an evacuation be organized, when communication is impossible and many of the residents cannot be reached? Also, many of them were injured or had already begun to suffer from illness and hunger as a result of the lack of supplies.

The scale of the devastation—and the immediate need for aid—are difficult to imagine. It was hard to know where and how to start helping. Other countries and nations began helping and delivering aid as soon as they could. However, because communications lines were down, things became chaotic. It became evident that the aid of supplies, food, and medical equipment promised by some nations was not reaching Managua.

In Puerto Rico, the Clemente family was enjoying the Christmas holiday together. The news of the quake in nearby Nicaragua, however, shocked them out of their cheerful holiday spirits. Roberto had spent a lot of time in Nicaragua, and he and Vera were fond of the country and its people.

"As soon as we heard about the earthquake early that morning we were very upset because we met some very nice people down there and felt like we [lost] someone—you know, a relative or someone," Vera Clemente recalled. "We felt very involved in this."[23]

They were frustrated, however, because the news out of Managua was hard to come by. The earthquake had cut major power lines so news and radio broadcasts were feeble and not very informative. Nobody really knew, in those first few days, how bad the situation on the ground in Managua really was. The devastation had also collapsed the headquarters of the city's major newspaper offices.

Clemente called a friend and talked about the quake. "What should we do?" he asked his friend, then quickly added, "I don't know what you're going to do, but I'm going to do something about it."[24] Later that night, Clemente and some friends, who were also celebrities in Puerto Rico, made some initial plans to lead a rescue effort to show the people of Nicaragua that the people of Puerto Rico cared about their plight. They formed the Comité Roberto Clemente Pro-Nicaragua, the Roberto Clemente Committee for Nicaragua.

While the Puerto Rican government had promised aid, Roberto Clemente felt that there was a lot of interference with the aid reaching Nicaragua. He decided that he and others had to adopt a more aggressive rescue mission.

FOILED BY CORRUPTION

The next day, members of this newly formed committee made a public announcement on Puerto Rican television, asking for people to bring donated supplies to the parking lot of Hiram Bithorn Stadium in San Juan. The plan was to lease an airplane and fly the supplies to Managua, to distribute them personally so that their arrival would be guaranteed. As it was the Christmas holiday, people in Puerto Rico were especially generous with their donations, wanting to help out their stricken neighbors across the Caribbean. The Senadores and the Cangrejeros had returned to their playing schedule and needed the use of Bithorn Stadium. Within a few days, the donation collection site had to be moved from the parking lot of the Hiram Bithorn Stadium to a larger lot across the street, at the Plaza Las Americas.

The first shipments sent by the Comité Roberto Clemente Pro-Nicaragua arrived a few days after the earthquake. They were flown in by Raul Pelligrina, a major in the National Guard. Volunteers had gathered in San Juan to load the airplane with the supplies that had been collected, including hospital equipment and medicines as well as food and clothing. Vera and Roberto Clemente watched the plane take off down the runway, feeling proud and satisfied. It would be the first of several shipments, hopefully, that they would send to Managua. When Major Pelligrina returned later that night to San Juan, however, the news he brought with him infuriated Clemente and the others on the relief committee: the supplies he had delivered probably never reached the people who really needed them. The problem was Nicaragua's leader, Anastasio Somoza Debayle.

Debayle's father, Anastasio Somoza Garcia, had been Nicaragua's president since 1937, the beginning of the Somoza political dynasty in that country. Known as Tacho, the elder Somoza was corrupt and crushed civil liberties in the nation. He was assassinated in 1956, after which his eldest son, Luis Somoza Debayle, was named president. Anastasio, the younger son, called "Tachito," or "little Tacho," played a large role in his brother's political rule.

On May 1, 1967, Tachito was elected the 44th president of Nicaragua, shortly before his elder brother died. Just as he shared his father's name, Tachito was very much like his father in his political philosophy: he ruled totally and as a dictator, not as an elected official. His term as president ended on May 1, 1972, but Somoza Debayle arranged for a three-person cabinet to succeed him until he was allowed, according to the constitution, to run again in 1974. However, in the intermittent two years, he would be the head of the National Guard, or the highest person in the military, which effectively meant that he ruled the country from the sidelines.

Somoza Debayle was officially the 44th and 45th president of Nicaragua, from May 1967 to May 1972 and from December 1974 to July 1979. When the December 1972 earthquake hit the country, martial law was declared, and, as head of the National Guard, he once again became ruler. As head of the national emergency relief committee, Somoza was widely accused of stealing aid sent to the country from abroad. In fact, to this day, parts of Managua have never been rebuilt.

When the earthquake hit on December 23, martial law was declared. As head of the National Guard, Somoza Debayle once again became the official leader of the country, to help order the relief effort and keep the situation under control.

However, as many people agreed, Somoza Debayle seemed more interested in profiting from the tragedy that struck

Managua than in helping the city, the nation, and the people to recover from it. Bianca Jagger, wife of Rolling Stones' lead singer Mick Jagger, arrived in Managua with her own plane of aid supplies. As a native of Nicaragua, she had been personally affected by the news of the quake. When she arrived at the airport, however, she was horrified by what she saw. As reported by David Maraniss, "Soldiers were everywhere, [Jagger] recalled in an interview with journalist Kurt Jacobsen, but they were just seizing supplies and taking them to government warehouses. Nearby, on the other side of the fences, hungry people were shouting for food and water, their pleas ignored. . . . She would never forget the arrogance of the Somoza regime, she said."[25]

Other reports had come in, testifying to the corruption of the Nicaraguan National Guard. Every day since the earthquake had hit, special envoys, carrying supplies and relief aid, had been flying into the country, but now it seemed that very little of that aid was actually reaching the people of Managua. The upper classes of Nicaragua were openly voicing their resentment of the Somoza regime, and the country's Catholic clergy were also vocal in their outrage over how Somoza and the military were exploiting the tragedy of the earthquake.

This is what Raul Pelligrina reported to Clemente and others. The mission seemed to be a bust. "The moment they landed," according to Maraniss, "Somoza's soldiers surrounded the plane and tried to take everything. Nicaragua was in chaos. No one knew whether aid was getting to the right people. Pelligrina, calling the military's bluff, said that if they did not let him through he would reload his aircraft and fly back to San Juan and tell the great Roberto Clemente what was happening."[26] After hearing this, the soldiers sent for Somoza Debayle's son, who agreed to let Pelligrina get through to Managua with his supplies. Had he not invoked the name of Clemente, however, Pelligrina knew he never

10

The Legacy of Roberto Clemente

Roberto Clemente and the members of the relief committee that bore his name had no way of knowing that the airplane they chartered had a troubled history. The committee members leased a DC-7 to carry the next cargo of supplies to Managua. The owner of the plane was Arthur Rivera, who owned several planes that were part of his business in which he imported and exported goods to the various islands in the Caribbean, including Puerto Rico.

Rivera himself had been in the hot seat with aviation officials. He had never obtained a commercial pilot's license, although he hauled goods across the Caribbean. The reason suspected for his failure to obtain the license is that he wanted to avoid the more rigorous cargo inspections that commercial air pilots have to undergo. In 1970, in fact, the Federal Aviation Administration in San Juan revoked Rivera's pilot's license, stating that his "aviation knowledge and experience was relatively limited."[27] The action was meant to stop Rivera from flying commercial flights without following the proper rules. Rivera appealed the revocation, which was eventually reduced by a court to a temporary suspension.

In July 1972, Rivera bought the DC-7, much larger than the other smaller planes he owned in Miami, but he had to hire a more experienced pilot to fly it back to San Juan for him because he did not know how to operate the plane. The old plane sat at the San Juan International Airport for several months, as its flying condition was doubtful. Rivera painted the outside of the plane to make it look newer, and he put out advertisements offering the plane for lease.

On December 2, 1972, Rivera and a copilot took the plane out for a test run. However, Rivera made a few errors in handling the aircraft, and the plane ended up crashing in a drainage ditch. The damage was substantial. According to Maraniss, the damage included "two blown tires, bent blades on the No. 2 and No. 3 propellers, sudden stoppage of the No. 2 and No. 3 engines, broken hydraulic lines on the right landing gear, and damage to the No. 3 engine oil scoop."[28] However, the mechanics hired by Rivera reassured him that despite what aviation inspectors said, the engines had not stopped and did not actually need to be replaced, which made the aircraft's owner quite happy—he would be saving a lot of money by not replacing the engines. He did, however, invest some money in repainting it and sprucing up the exterior again.

Arthur Rivera and Roberto Clemente met when Clemente and his wife, Vera, were at the San Juan International Airport. They were supervising the loading of supplies onto the plane piloted by Raul Pelligrina for its next flight to Managua. Rivera's mechanic spotted Clemente and offered to show him the DC-7, which looked spotless and reliable with its fresh coat of paint. Clemente met Rivera, who offered the plane for lease for an extra run to Managua. For $4,000, Rivera said, he would assemble a crew and make a flight to Nicaragua, staying as long as Clemente needed to remain there. The two men shook hands on the deal, planning to leave the next day, December 31.

Clemente was excited. What he did not realize was that Arthur Rivera himself still did not know how to fly the DC-7, and so Rivera was looking desperately to find a pilot who could. At the airport, he was making inquiries when he happened to meet Jerry Hill, an American pilot who saw the DC-7 and made a chance comment: "I used to fly one of these."[29] Without further questioning, Rivera hired him on the spot. Had he bothered to investigate, he would have learned that while Hill was an experienced pilot, he had committed 13 violations of aviation policy and was, at the time, at risk of losing his commercial pilot's license.

The other crew members consisted of Rivera himself, who would copilot the plane, and Francisco Matias, another mechanic who had helped fix up the plane after it crashed into the drainage ditch weeks earlier. Clemente would also be on board, of course, as well as Angel Lozana, a colleague of Clemente's and a member of the relief committee.

Meanwhile, Roberto Clemente had decided he would be on the flight himself because Somoza's soldiers continued to give Pelligrina problems, obstructing the delivery of much-needed supplies. They would not dare to tangle with the great Roberto Clemente, one of Latin America's superstars. As always, Clemente's priority was to get help to those who needed it, even if that meant inconveniencing himself. The plane was loaded with supplies on the afternoon of December 31, and it quickly became apparent that the plane was actually being overloaded. The DC-7 was capable of carrying a maximum of 40,000 pounds (18 metric tons), but the cargo exceeded that maximum by at least 4,000 pounds (1.8 metric tons).

Roberto said good-bye to his wife and climbed aboard. The plane, however, was delayed by several hours because of a malfunction. The pilot and several mechanics worked busily to fix the problem, a set of bad sparkplugs, and then resumed the plan for takeoff. It seemed that one final omen, a sign not to make the fateful journey, had been ignored.

NEVER RECOVERED

As the plane made its way down the runway, as many eyewitnesses later testified, it seemed that it was having trouble gathering the needed momentum and speed to take off. A few people heard several loud, backfiring noises right before the plane ascended into the air. Within a few minutes of the plane's takeoff, air traffic controllers knew it was in trouble. As it made its way above the water, it suddenly disappeared off the radar screen.

Controllers immediately gave out the signal for help: a DC-7 had apparently crashed into the waters off the coast of San Juan. The U.S. Coast Guard and the Navy began a rescue mission, hoping to find and save the five occupants on board. Yet in the dark waters on that New Year's Eve, their mission seemed impossible. Before long, as the search continued with no luck, the effort switched to a recovery mission, as they attempted to find the wreckage and the bodies of those men who were now presumed dead.

Vera Clemente received word from Roberto's niece on the telephone, and she rushed immediately to the home of her in-laws, Melchor and Luisa. The elderly couple was devastated, and the family then hurried to the airport to find out the exact details of what was happening.

The recovery effort lasted several days. Two days after the plane went down, the Coast Guard and Navy, along with many volunteers, eventually began to find some of the debris from the crash, including Angel Lozano's wallet and, later, Roberto's briefcase. A day later, the badly broken body of pilot Jerry Hill was found. Still a couple of days later, actual parts of the plane were discovered, including parts of the engine, cockpit, a wing, and the tail section.

The reason the plane went down, officials later determined, was that the faulty engines—which Rivera had never

Roberto Clemente's DC-7, loaded with supplies for the victims of the Nicaraguan earth-quake, crashed into the waters off San Juan, Puerto Rico, on December 31, 1972. All five people aboard, including Clemente, died in the crash. Here U.S. Navy divers inspect the debris of the plane, 120 feet (37 meters) down on the ocean floor.

replaced, despite being advised to do so—had been over-loaded. The pilot, Jerry Hill, had pushed them too hard, and the engines were unable to stand up to the pressure and had failed. The tragedy of it all, of course, is that it could have been prevented. The life of one of the world's greatest humanitarians had been snuffed out because of greediness over a business transaction.

Roberto Clemente's body and the bodies of three others on board—Lozano, Matias, and Rivera—were never found. For Vera Clemente, who had spent every morning during the search and recovery waiting on the shore, this was probably the greatest tragedy of the whole situation. She and Roberto's three sons, parents, siblings, and extended family mourned the fact that they did not have his body to bury.

In Pittsburgh, where Roberto Clemente was just as much of an idol as he was in his native Puerto Rico, shocked fans mourned for their hero. In Mount Washington, writes David Maraniss, lights spelled out the words, "Adios, Amigo Roberto."[30] A simple but sad message, it was the way the whole world seemed to feel at the loss of such a man.

THE LEGEND BEGINS

"That night on which Roberto Clemente left us physically, his immortality began," wrote Elliott Castro, a writer from Puerto Rico. The legend of Roberto Clemente began almost as soon as his DC-7, on a mission of mercy, crashed into the sea near San Juan.

The shoreline near the San Juan International Airport was lined with people who flocked to the site to watch and pray during the search and recovery mission. Newspapers anxiously reported every detail of the recovery effort; the news of the effort even overshadowed the inauguration of Puerto Rico's new governor, whose inaugural ceremony, which was very somber, seemed to be dedicated to Roberto Clemente.

Many people continued to hope that Roberto Clemente was alive. Perhaps he had made his way to land somewhere, people wondered, or was floating somewhere in the sea, barely alive. When the first week was over, however, it was obvious to all that Clemente was gone, his glorious life and career swept away by a series of petty deceits and errors.

The next challenge was how best to honor such an amazing man. The Baseball Writers Association of America had one answer. The Baseball Hall of Fame in Cooperstown has a rule stating that a player cannot be inducted into its hallowed halls until five years after his retirement from the sport. Yet in the wake of the tragedy of Clemente's death, it seemed unnecessary to follow the waiting period guideline. Clemente's career had been a marvelous one, and there was no question of his eligibility in terms of talent. A vote was taken, and of the 424 writers who voted, 93 percent voted for his early induction, making Roberto Clemente the first Latino baseball player to be admitted to the Hall of Fame. The ceremony took place on August 6, 1973, with Vera accepting the award in Roberto's honor.

THE ROBERTO CLEMENTE SPORTS CITY

When he won the National League's MVP Award in 1966, Clemente publicly said, "'Before I came here, you never had many outstanding players from the Caribbean. There were some good ones and now I won the MVP. This makes me happy because now I feel that if I could do it, then they could do it. The kids have someone to look up to and to follow. I show them what baseball has done for me, and maybe they will work harder and try harder and be better men."[31]

Clemente had a plan to show the kids of Puerto Rico that they too could have a career in baseball. Yet for most of his life, that plan remained an elusive dream. The dream, one he spoke about constantly to his wife and in public speeches, finally came true after his tragic death. The Roberto Clemente Sports City, a 304-acre complex, was built in his hometown of Carolina, Puerto Rico, and it is currently managed by Vera Clemente and two of her sons, Luis Roberto Clemente and Enrique Roberto Clemente. It features a baseball stadium, a running track, playing fields, a gymnasium, basketball courts, tennis courts, and a swimming pool, and it is open for the children of the island to come and play and practice. Each year, it hosts over 200,000 young people in its programs and facilities.

Even professional players use it to practice for competitions. The Sports City has harvested many excellent major league players, including Ruben Sierra, Roberto Alomar, and Sandy Alomar.

ON-AND-OFF-THE-FIELD EXCELLENCE

In June 2007, Gary Sheffield of the Detroit Tigers commented in an article in *GQ Magazine* that Latin-American baseball players are easier to control than African-American players. "I called it years ago," he said. "What I called is that you're going to see more black faces, but there ain't no English going to be coming out. . . . [It's about] being able to tell [Latin players] what to do, being able to control them."

Sheffield implied that Latino players could be controlled by intimidation, the fear that they would be sent back to their native countries if they did not follow what baseball administrators told them to do. Sheffield, an African American, was giving voice to a common complaint about the dominating presence of Latinos in Major League Baseball and to the shrinking numbers of African Americans in the sport.

His comment that Major League Baseball could control Latin-American players more easily than African-American players ignited a controversy, as sportswriters and fans debated the accuracy of Sheffield's points.

It is interesting to ponder how Roberto Clemente would have responded to the comments. Indeed, when Clemente first joined the ranks of the Pittsburgh Pirates, not many major league players could claim Spanish as their native language. Clemente struggled with the American sports media because he felt they disrespected him as a Latin American and because his skin was dark. He objected, for example, when he was referred to as "Bob," insisting that he be called "Roberto." Indeed, Clemente may have agreed that because he was a Latino, he experienced somewhat more pressure than white players, especially since he played during the Jim Crow era of segregation in the United States.

POSTHUMOUS AWARDS

David Maraniss calculates that, since Clemente's death, "Forty public schools, two hospitals, and more than two hundred parks and ballfields bear his name, from Carolina, Puerto

However, Sheffield's comment to *GQ Magazine* is another illustration of how far Latin-American players have come in Major League Baseball. Most major league ball clubs actively recruit in the Caribbean islands, especially in Puerto Rico and the Dominican Republic, to find the best new talents. Some of the game's biggest stars in the last ten years have been Latin American, from Bernie Williams and Sammy Sosa to Pedro Martinez and Alex Rodriguez. Currently, baseball players of Latino heritage make up approximately 30 percent of the rosters of major league ball clubs, making them the most widely represented ethnic minority in the sport. African Americans currently comprise less than ten percent of the baseball rosters in the major leagues.

The Baseball Hall of Fame, however, has inducted only six other players of Latino heritage to its hallowed halls so far: these include Martin Dihigo, Juan Marichal, Luis Aparicio, Rod Carew, Orlando Cepeda, and Tony Perez, who hail from places as diverse as Panama, Venezuela, the Dominican Republic, Puerto Rico, and Cuba.

Of course Clemente was the first—part of his legacy is that he set the standard for those who came after him. His excellence on and off the field ensured that Latin-American players would be considered among baseball's elite by fans and sportswriters alike.

One aspect of Clemente's legacy, however, will be difficult for anyone to emulate: his passion for humanitarian issues. Roberto Clemente considered his baseball career to be a platform for him to call attention to major international issues, such as poverty and hunger in Latin America. He used his fame to improve the lives of others, and while many baseball players today lend their names to charitable causes, it is not easy to find an example of a player who does so with the enthusiasm and passion that Clemente did.

On July 12, 1994, a 12-foot (3.6-meter) bronze statue of Roberto Clemente was dedicated at Three Rivers Stadium. In 2001, the statue was move to the Pirates' new home, PNC Park. Clemente is remembered not only for his ethnic pride and for using his baseball career to better the lives of Latin Americans but also for his work to make the world a happier and fairer place.

Rico, where he was born, to Pittsburgh, Pennsylvania, where he played, to far-off Mannheim, Germany."[32]

Some of the awards named in honor of Clemente have been most suitable in terms of recognizing charitable works. Major League Baseball honors players who contribute to their communities as well as play outstandingly on the field. Since 1973, the year after Clemente died, that award has been named the Roberto Clemente Man of the Year Award. Each ball club selects a local honoree, and from that pool of nominees, a national winner is selected and the award presented at the World Series. Past winners have included Rod Carew, Greg Luzinski, Cal Ripken Jr., Kirby Puckett, Sammy Sosa, and Edgar Martinez.

Martinez, who won the award in 2004, said, "I never saw [Clemente] play, other than on television in the 1971 World Series, but I heard so much about him from people who did see him play. They talked about the way he played the game. That is why this award means so much to me. It is more about making a contribution off the field instead of on the field."[33]

LATINO PLAYERS IN BASEBALL TODAY

Since Roberto Clemente graced the outfield at Three Rivers Stadium in a Pirates uniform, many Latino players have also participated in America's national pastime. Many compare the rise of Latino players to that of African-American players since Jackie Robinson integrated the sport in 1947. Robinson played for the Brooklyn Dodgers, the team that initially signed Clemente, and his breakthrough season in 1947 opened the doors for other ball clubs to sign other African-American players. While Clemente was not the first Latin-American player to appear in the major leagues, he was certainly the most well known, and during and since his spectacular career, other young Latino hopefuls have made their way onto the baseball diamond.

As many as 30 percent of the players in professional baseball today are of Latin-American descent, according to some estimates. Many of those players hail from Cuba and Puerto Rico as well as other places in Latin America, where Clemente's name still invokes a sense of awe. "Every single kid in Puerto Rico knows who he was—a great guy, a great player, a man who helped everybody," said Edgard Velasquez, Clemente's nephew who played for the Colorado Rockies. "He represented all Latino players. There was only Roberto."[34]

Chronology

1934   Roberto Clemente Walker born August 18 in Carolina, Puerto Rico; he is the youngest of four children of Melchor Clemente and Luisa Walker.

1952   Signed as the youngest player, at the age of 18, to play for the Santurce Cangrejeros.

1953   The Brooklyn Dodgers sign the 19-year-old for a $5,000 first-year salary and a $10,000 bonus.

1954   Frustrated by a lack of playing time with Brooklyn's Triple-A minor league team in Montreal, gets a big break when Pittsburgh selects him as the number-one pick in Major League Baseball's annual postseason draft.

1955   On April 17, makes his major league debut with the Pittsburgh Pirates, in a game against the Brooklyn Dodgers.

1956   Bats .311, the first of 13 times he will bat over .300.

1934
Roberto Clemente Walker born August 18 in Carolina, Puerto Rico

1960
Pittsburgh Pirates win World Series for the first time in 25 years

1934

1964

1953
Signed by Brooklyn Dodgers for a $5,000 first-year salary and a $10,000 bonus

1964
Marries Vera Christina Zabala, a native of Carolina, Puerto Rico

1960   The Pirates win the World Series; bats .310, with four RBI, helping Pittsburgh to their first world championship in 35 years; named a National League All-Star for the first time, the first of 12 such honors.

1961   Wins the first of 12 consecutive Gold Glove Awards, with a career-high 27 assists; wins the first of four batting titles, hitting .351; leads the league again in 1964 (.339), 1965 (.329), and 1967 (.357).

1964   Marries Vera Christina Zabala, also a native of Carolina, Puerto Rico; leads National League in hits with 211.

1965   Diagnosed with malaria and is hospitalized.

1967   Leads National League in hits with 209.

1966   Named National League Most Valuable Player of the National League; finishes the season with a .317 batting average, 29 home runs, and 119 RBI.

1966
Named Most
Valuable Player
of the National
League

1972
Gets his 3,000th hit, the last base hit of his great career. Dies in a plane crash off the coast of San Juan, en route to Managua, Nicaragua, to deliver medical supplies and food to earthquake-ravaged survivors

1966

1973

1971
Named Most
Valuable Player of
the World Series

1973
Inducted
into the
Baseball
Hall of Fame

1971 Pirates defeat Baltimore Orioles to win the World Series; named World Series Most Valuable Player, batting .414 with 12 hits, two home runs, and three RBI.

1972 On September 30, gets his 3,000th hit; it will be the last hit of his regular-season career. On October 11, plays in his last Major League Baseball game, in the National League Championship Series, against the Cincinnati Reds.

On December 31, dies in a plane crash off the coast of San Juan, en route to Managua, Nicaragua, to deliver medical supplies and food to survivors of a massive earthquake that occurred the previous week.

1973 Less than three months after his death, is voted into the Baseball Hall of Fame in Cooperstown, New York, on March 20, and is formally inducted on August 6, the first Hispanic player ever elected; at the ceremony, baseball commissioner Bowie Kuhn announces the creation of the Roberto Clemente Award, baseball's highest award for sportsmanship and community activism.

Notes

Chapter 2

1 Quoted in David Maraniss, *Clemente: The Passion and Grace of Baseball's Last Hero* (New York: Simon and Schuster, 2006), p 18.
2 Ibid., 18.
3 Ibid., 21–22.
4 Ibid., 25.

Chapter 3

5 Ibid.
6 Ibid., 26.
7 Ibid., 27.
8 Ibid., 37.
9 Ibid., 44.

Chapter 8

10 Quoted in Bruce Markusen, *Roberto Clemente: The Great One* (Champaign, IL: Sagamore Publishing, 1998), 183.
11 Quoted in Paul Robert Walker, *Pride of Puerto Rico: The Life of Roberto Clemente* (New York: Odyssey Classics, 1991), 128.
12 Ibid., 131.
13 Markusen, 242.
14 Ibid., 250.
15 Walker, *Pride*, 133–134.
16 Ibid., 136.
17 Ibid., 138.
18 Ibid., 142–143.

Chapter 9

19 Maraniss, *The Passion and Grace*, 266.
20 Ibid., 267.

21 Ibid.
22 Ibid., 289.
23 Ibid., 291.
24 Ibid., 295.
25 Ibid., 303.
26 Ibid., 302.

Chapter 10

27 Ibid., 311.
28 Ibid., 315.
29 Ibid., 319.
30 Ibid., 336.
31 Smithsonian Institute, "Beyond Baseball: The Life of Roberto Clemente/His Story/Sports City and Other Dreams." Available online. URL: http://www.robertoclemente.si.edu/english/virtual_story_sports_08.htm.
32 Maraniss, 2.
33 Smithsonian Institute, "Beyond Baseball: The Life of Roberto Clemente." Available online. URL: www.robertoclemente.si.edu/english/virtual_story_boyhood_01.htm.
34 Patrick Ridgell, "A Touch of Royalty in Right Field: Baseball Player Roberto Clemente." *Latino Leaders: The National Magazine of the Successful American Latino,* February–March 2002. Retrieved June 1, 2007, from http://findarticles.com/p/articles/mi_m0PCH/is_1_3/ai_113053518.

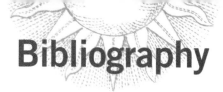

Bibliography

Books

Kingsbury, Robert. *Roberto Clemente.* New York: Rosen Publishing, 2003.

Maraniss, David. *Clemente: The Passion and Grace of Baseball's Last Hero.* New York: Simon and Schuster, 2006.

Markusen, Bruce. *Roberto Clemente: The Great One.* Champaign, IL: Sagamore Publishing, 1998.

Walker, Paul Robert. *Pride of Puerto Rico: The Life of Roberto Clemente.* New York: Odyssey Classics, 1991.

Newspapers, Magazines, and Web sites

Answers.com "Roberto Clemente." Available online. URL: www. answers.com/topic/roberto-clemente.

The National Magazine of the Successful American Latino

"On This Day: 1972: Earthquake Wreaks Devastation in Nicaragua." bbc.co.uk. Available online. URL: http://news.bbc.co.uk/onthisday/ hi/dates/stories/december/23/newsid_2540000/2540045.stm.

Ridgell, Patrick. "A Touch of Royalty in Right Field: Baseball Player Roberto Clemente." *Latino Leaders: The National Magazine of the Successful American Latino,* February–March 2002. Retrieved June 1, 2007, from http://findarticles.com/p/articles/mi_m0PCH/ is_1_3/ai_113053518.

Smithsonian Institute. "Beyond Baseball: The Life of Roberto Clemente." Available online. URL: http://www.robertoclemente. si.edu/english/virtual_story_boyhood_01.htm.

Sporting News

Thornley, Stew. Society for American Baseball Research, BIOPROJ.SABR.ORG.

"Roberto Clemente." Available online. URL: http://bioproj.sabr.org/ bioproj.cfm?a=v&v=l&bid=1255&pid=2553.

Wikipedia. "Roberto Clemente." Available online. URL: http://en.wikipedia.org/wiki/Roberto_Clemente.

Further Reading

Bjarkman, Peter. *Baseball with a Latin Beat: A History of the Latin American Game.* Jefferson, N.C.: McFarland & Company, 1994.

Breton, Marcos. *Home Is Everything: The Latino Baseball Story: From the Barrio to the Major Leagues.* El Paso, Tex.: Cinco Puntos Press, 2003.

Engel, Trudie. *We'll Never Forget You, Roberto Clemente.* New York: Scholastic Paperbacks, 1997.

Wagenheim, Karl. *Clemente!* Chicago: Olmstead Press, 2001.

Web sites

Smithsonian Institute, Beyond Baseball: The Roberto Clemente Story
www.robertoclemente.si.edu/english/index.htm

Latino Legends in Sports
www.latinosportslegends.com/stats/baseball/Clemente_Roberto-career_stats_highlights.htm

The Roberto Clemente Sports City Official Web site
www.rcsc21.com/

Latino Baseball
www.latinobaseball.com/index.php

Picture Credits

page:

Index

About the Author

Rob Maaddi is the Philadelphia sports editor/writer for The Associated Press. He is also the host of "The Rob Maaddi Show" weekly on ESPN 920 radio in Philadelphia.

Susan Muaddi Darraj is associate professor of English at Harford Community College in Bel Air, Maryland. She is also the author of *The Inheritance of Exile*, published by University of Notre Dame Press.